LOST EMPIRES
ANCIENT AZTEC AND MAYA

LOST EMPIRES
ANCIENT AZTEC AND MAYA

The extraordinary history of 3000 years of Mesoamerican
civilization with over 270 photographs and illustrations

Charles Phillips
CONSULTANT: Dr David M Jones

southwater

This edition is published by Southwater

Southwater is an imprint of Anness Publishing Ltd
Hermes House, 88–89 Blackfriars Road, London SE1 8HA
tel. 020 7401 2077; fax 020 7633 9499
www.southwaterbooks.com; info@anness.com

© Anness Publishing Ltd 2005

UK agent: The Manning Partnership Ltd
tel. 01225 478444; fax 01225 478440
sales@manning-partnership.co.uk

UK distributor: Grantham Book Services Ltd
tel. 01476 541080; fax 01476 541061; orders@gbs.tbs-ltd.co.uk

North American agent/distributor: National Book Network
tel. 301 459 3366; fax 301 429 5746; www.nbnbooks.com

Australian agent/distributor: Pan Macmillan Australia
tel. 1300 135 113; fax 1300 135 103
customer.service@macmillan.com.au

New Zealand agent/distributor: David Bateman Ltd
tel. (09) 415 7664; fax (09) 415 8892

A CIP catalogue record for this book is available from
the British Library.

Publisher: Joanna Lorenz
Editorial Director: Helen Sudell
Editors: Joy Wotton and Elizabeth Woodland
Designer: Nigel Partridge
Cover Designer: Adelle Morris
Maps: Peter Bull Art Studio
Illustrations: Vanessa Card
Production Controller: Wendy Lawson
Editorial Reader: Jay Thundercliffe

Previously published as part of a larger volume, *The Illustrated
Encyclopedia of Aztec and Maya*

10 9 8 7 6 5 4 3 2 1

Page 1, Aerial of Rain Forest. Page 2, Steep stairs ascend the
Temple of the Count at the Maya city of Palenque.
Page 3, A pre-Columbian Figure in Oaxaca, Mexico.
Page 4, Chichén Itzá. Page 5, Chac Mool Mayan Figure.

CONTENTS

INTRODUCTION

In 1519, a group of Spanish soldiers on an exploratory voyage from the Spanish colony in Cuba encountered a great civilization in full flower in the Valley of Mexico. From a cold mountain pass between the awe-inspiring snow-capped peaks of Popocatépetl and Ixtaccíhuatl, the nervous Spaniards looked down on a remarkable series of interconnected lakes in the Valley, with well-ordered towns and raised fields on the shores, and a great city built on islands and causeways towards the western edge of the largest of the lakes. They knew something of the Aztec people who built this city, Tenochtitlán, for earlier in the adventure the Spaniards had encountered the Aztecs' allies and enemies and heard tales of their vast empire. As the Spaniards marched down on to the plain and neared the city, they went across one of the causeways linking the island metropolis to the mainland and were astounded by

Below: The builders of Maya cities such as Tikal, in Guatemala, raised towering stone temples in the midst of thick jungle.

Tenochtitlán's size and beauty. The great temples and palaces rose from the water like a vision. One member of the Spanish force, Bernal Díaz del Castillo, later likened it to a city from a fairytale, a vision of enchantment.

EARLY BEGINNINGS
The city of Tenochtitlán and the culture of its Aztec builders was the product of more than 22,000 years of human activity, which stretched back to the arrival of the first hunter-gatherers in America in 21,000BC.

Descendants of these ancient settlers who left their mark in the area included the Olmec builders of the great cities of La Venta and San Lorenzo in *c.*1200BC, the Zapotec architects of Monte Albán in *c.*500BC and the Toltec founders of Tollán in AD950. They also included the Maya, who built their remarkable jungle cities in the lands to the east of the Valley of Mexico in the first centuries of the Christian era. At the time of the Conquest they were still thriving in the northern part of the Yucatán peninsula.

Above: Mictlantecuhtli, the Aztec 'Lord of the Dead', was worshipped in this form by the people of Teotihuacán in c.100BC.

WHAT WAS MESOAMERICA?
Scholars give the name Mesoamerica to this 22,000-year timespan and to the lands settled by these peoples; it is both a cultural and a geographical label. Geographically, Mesoamerica runs from the area of desert north of the Valley of Mexico across Guatemala and Honduras to western Nicaragua and Costa Rica.

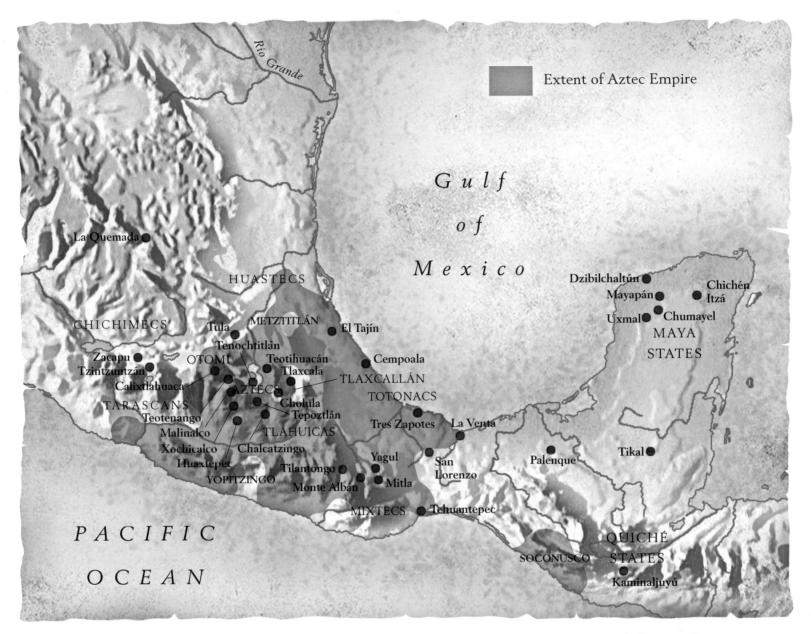

Río Grande

Extent of Aztec Empire

Gulf
of
Mexico

HUASTECS

La Quemada

CHICHIMECS   Tula   METZTITLÁN   El Tajín

Zacapu   OTOMÍ   Teotihuacán   Cempoala

Tenochtitlán

Tzintzuntzán   Tlaxcala

Calixtlahuaca   AZTECS   TLAXCALLÁN

TARASCANS   Cholula   TOTONACS

Teotenango   Tepoztlán   Tres Zapotes   La Venta

Malinalco

Xochicalco   TLAHUICAS

Huaxtepec   Chalcatzingo   Yagul

YOPITZINGO   Tilantongo   San
Lorenzo

Monte Albán   Mitla

MIXTECS   Tehuantepec

PACIFIC

OCEAN

Dzibilchaltún   Chichén
Mayapán   Itzá
Uxmal   Chumayel

MAYA
STATES

Palenque   Tikal

QUICHÉ
SOCONUSCO   STATES

Kaminaljuyú

Above: Map showing the main sites of the successive Mesoamerican cultures and the size of the Aztec empire in 1510.

It largely coincides with what we call Middle America, including areas of some modern Central American countries. Other Central American countries, such as Panama, were not settled by Mesoamericans. Mexico, most of which was an important part of Mesoamerica, is geographically part of North America. Historically, Mesoamerica covers all events between the arrival of the first human settlers in the region in *c*.21,000BC and the Conquest of the Mesoamerican empire in 1521.

Scholars use an additional set of chronological divisions to divide Maya history. The years *c*.AD250–900 that represent the fullest flowering of Maya civilization are labelled the Classic Period. The Classic years are the ones in which the Maya set up dated stone columns celebrating the achievements of their holy kings. The 20,000-odd years before are called the Archaic (20,000–*c*.2500BC) and Preclassic (*c*.2500BC– AD250) periods. The 600-odd years after are known as the Postclassic Period (AD900–1500s).

This book covers the historical achievements and mythology of all these cultures, concentrating on the cultures of the Maya and the Aztecs because we know most about them. Succeeding cultures inherited a great deal from their predecessors.

Right: Tall stone warrior figures carved by Toltec craftsmen in the 11th century AD celebrated a fierce, militaristic culture.

Religious rituals, cultural achievements and mythological elements are common to most of the peoples of the Mesoamerican region and historical period, so that it is possible to talk of 'Mesoamerican civilization'.

CALENDARS

Foremost among these common elements was the use of a complex ritual calendar. Among the Maya and Aztecs, priests marked the passing of time and predicted the future with two calendars, one a solar count of 365 days linked to the passing seasons, another a ritual calendar of 260 days, thought to be based on the length of a human pregnancy. The two calendars combined to make a longer measure. The period needed for a particular day in the 365-day calendar and a particular day in the 260-day calendar to coincide was 18,980 days, or 52 365-day years. This measure, called the 'bundle of years' by the Aztecs, was invested with great

Above: This court in Xochicalco, Mexico, was built in AD700–800 for playing the ball game revered by Mesoamericans.

significance. The end of each 52-year period was seen as a moment of great danger, at which the gods might end the world. The preoccupation with measuring and recording time went far back into Mesoamerican history – the earliest surviving writing from the region may be a Zapotec calendrical note from *c*.600BC – and the calendar was very widely used throughout the region. Indeed, the scholar Michael Coe has suggested that one good way of defining Mesoamerica would be to draw a line around the area known to have used the ritual calendar.

BLOOD SACRIFICE

Another important central element of Mesoamerican civilization – at least as far back as the Olmecs in *c*.1200BC – was the use of human blood sacrifice to honour and propitiate the gods. Among the Aztecs, vast lines of prisoners of

Left: The long-nosed Maya rain god Chac – carved here at Sayil, Mexico – had his counterpart in Tláloc, the Aztec god of rain.

war were paraded up steep temple pyramids to be sacrificed by having their hearts ripped from their chests. The Classic-Period Maya more commonly decapitated their victims. Both Maya and Aztec worshippers also offered their own blood to the gods. Women and men drew blood from wounds in their cheeks, ears, arms and legs while men also made cuts in the penis.

The Mesoamericans worshipped a vast pantheon of gods and goddesses in the course of their civilization. These deities often have alternative names and animal or human twin forms. The cult of one god in particular was enduringly popular across centuries and cultures. The Plumed Serpent Quetzalcóatl, known to the Maya as Kukulcán, was associated with wise rulership and revered as a creator, a wind god and as the morning star. In myth, he was said to have departed by sea on a raft of snakes, promising to return. It is a popular theory that some among the Aztecs may have interpreted the coming of Hernán Cortés and his Spanish troops in 1519 as the promised return of Quetzalcóatl from exile.

THE BALL COURT

One of the basic common elements of Mesoamerican civilization was a ball game played on a court shaped like a capital 'I'. The court, which formed part of the ritual

complex in cities, had sloping or vertical side walls. The object appears to have been to get the ball into the end sections, rather like the 'endzones' on an American football pitch or the areas where tries are scored on a British rugby pitch. Some courts had rings high on the side walls and extra points may have been scored by getting the ball through the hoop. This would have been difficult since players

Left: Tezcatlipoca played a part in the ball game as an enactment of cosmic struggles.

Above: On the steep steps of temples, the Aztecs made human sacrifices to the gods.

could not direct the ball with their feet or hands, only their hips, elbows and knees. The game seems to have been understood as an enactment of cosmic struggles; by the Aztecs as a clash between light and dark, between Quetzalcóatl and his dark brother Tezcatlipoca, by the Maya as a re-enactment of the myth cycle in which the Hero Twins go to the underworld to overcome the gods of that fearsome realm.

TIMELINE OF MESOAMERICA

Above: Stepped temple-pyramids at Monte Albán give on to a large plaza.

21,000BC Hunter-gatherers enter the New World across the Bering Strait and a few thousand years later live in the Valley of Mexico near where the Aztecs will build their capital, Tenochtitlán.

7000–5000BC Mesoamerican settlers develop farming skills and domesticate wild plants – including maize.

2500–1500BC The first farming villages in Mesoamerica appear. Settlers raise maize, chilli peppers, squash and cotton.

1500–1200BC Olmecs build San Lorenzo.

1350BC A major urban settlement is built at San José Mogote.

1100BC A second Olmec city is built at La Venta.

1000BC The Ocós and Cuadros village-farming cultures thrive on the Pacific coast of Guatemala.

900BC The Olmec site of San Lorenzo is destroyed.

800BC Settlers build the first villages in the lowland Maya region.

600BC Carving on a monument at San José Mogote may be the earliest Mesoamerican writing.

*c.*600–400BC Maya build a living and ceremonial centre at Nakbé.

*c.*500BC Zapotecs build Monte Albán.

*c.*400BC The Olmec site of La Venta, on the Gulf coast, is destroyed. In the Valley of Mexico, Cuicuilco becomes an important city.

300BC Decline sets in at Nakbé.

300BC–AD100 Maya craftsmen build ceremonial and living centres at Tikal and Uaxactún, northern Guatemala.

*c.*100BC Volcanic eruption drives settlers from Cuicuilco, Valley of Mexico, to the city of Teotihuacán.

36BC The earliest Pre-Maya Long Count inscription is carved at Chiapa de Corzo in the Chiapas region of southern Mexico.

AD150 The Pyramid of the Sun is built at Teotihuacán.

AD199 The Hauberg stela, the earliest piece of writing in the Maya system, is carved.

AD200 The Zapotecs are at the peak of their powers.

Above: Temples at Palenque stand in the forested foothills of the Sierra Madre.

c. AD300–650 Peak of Maya building: pyramids, temples and ballcourts are put up in many Maya lowland cities.

c. AD350 Teotihuacán becomes the pre-eminent Mesoamerican city.

c. AD400 Copán expands from a farming settlement to a major city.

c. AD750 Northern tribes sack Teotihuacán.

AD700–900 Decline in Maya lowlands is perhaps caused by overpopulation.

AD799 Last stela carved in Palenque.

c. AD800 Murals painted at Bonampak.

AD820 Last dated stela is put up at Copán.

AD879 Last dated stela at Tikal.

c. AD850–950 Many Maya centres in Guatemala and Mexico are abandoned.

POSTCLASSIC PERIOD AD900–1521

AD 900–950 The Toltecs build their capital at Tula.

c.1000 Mixtec people carry out royal burials at Monte Albán.

c.1150 The city of Tula is destroyed by Chichimec tribesmen.

c.1200 The México/Aztecs make their way southward into the Valley of Mexico.

1263 The city of Mayapán is founded.

1325 The México/Aztecs found the city of Tenochtitlán.

Below: Toltec stone warriors at Tollán were originally painted in bright colours.

1375 Acamapichtli, the first historical ruler of the México/Aztecs, is elected *tlatoani* ('speaker') in Tenochtitlán.

1428 The cities of Tenochtitlán, Texcoco and Tlacopán form the Triple Alliance and begin to build the Aztec Empire.

1441 Mayapán falls and is abandoned.

1481 The Aztec Sun Stone is erected in Tenochtitlán.

1487 Ahuitzotl, *tlatoani* in Tenochtitlán, oversees the rededication of the city's Great Temple.

1492 Spanish explorers land in the West Indies.

1502 Christopher Columbus meets Maya traders in the Gulf of Honduras.

1502 Moctezuma II, the last independent Aztec ruler, becomes *tlatoani* in Tenochtitlán.

1507 A new 52-year cycle begins for the Aztecs with a New Fire ceremony.

1517 The first of three Spanish exploratory missions to Mesoamerica from Cuba is led by Francisco Hernández de Córdoba.

1519 Spanish explorers, led by Hernán Cortés, land in Mexico.

1521 Tenochtitlán falls to Cortés and his Spanish troops on 13 August after a siege of 93 days.

Above: The Aztec Sun Stone is an ancient calendar revealing much about the past.

1523–4 Spanish under Pedro de Alvarado conquer southern Maya lands in the highlands of Chiapas and in southern Guatemala.

c.1550 Members of the nobility among the Quiché, a group of southern Maya, secretly translate the Maya sacred book *Popol Vuh* ('Book of Advice') into the Roman alphabet in a bid to save it from the book-burning zeal of Spanish monks.

1566 Bishop Diego de Landa completes his *Report of Things of Yucatán*.

1569 Friar Bernardino de Sahagún completes his *General History of the Things of New Spain*.

1697 The last independent Maya centre – at Tayasal, on an island in Lake Flores, Guatemala – falls to the Spanish.

1703 Quiché-speaking Franciscan friar Francisco Ximenez finds *Popol Vuh* and translates it into Spanish.

1790 The Aztec Sun Stone is discovered in Mexico City.

CHAPTER ONE

3,000 YEARS OF CIVILIZATION

Civilization was born in the lands of Mesoamerica when the region's early farmers began to settle in villages around 2500–1500BC. The ancestors of these first villagers had spent perhaps 5,000 years in more or less nomadic farming and many millennia as hunter-gatherers. However, they took very quickly to the settled life and within a few centuries a major culture had arisen in the fertile, low-lying lands of Veracruz and Tabasco, adjoining the Gulf of Mexico. The creators of the Olmec civilization produced corn, squashes and other foodstuffs in such quantities that they could divert their energies into building and artistic activities. At La Venta and San Lorenzo they left behind large and impressive ceremonial centres and enigmatic carvings in stone. They laid the foundations for the great Mesoamerican civilization that would follow them: their pyramids, open plazas and rites of human sacrifice can all be found among the Zapotec, Teotihuacano, Toltec, Maya and Aztec societies that came in their wake. Other aspects of Mesoamerican religious and cultural life, including a deep reverence for the fleet-footed jaguar, were also first seen in Olmec lands. The essentials of a civilization that would endure for 3,000 years until the sudden and bloody arrival from the east of Hernán Cortés appear to have been laid in just a few hundred years by the inventive Olmec.

Left: Grass and stunted trees grow at high altitude beneath the vast, magnificent Popocatépetl. Rising 5,452m (17,900ft) above sea level, the volcano dominates the Valley of Mexico, where a succession of Mesoamerican cultures flourished.

THE BIRTH OF THE OLMEC

The first inhabitants of Mexico were probably descendants of Siberian immigrants to North America. Scholars do not know for sure when the first nomads arrived in the region we call Mesoamerica, but radiocarbon dating of bone fragments found at Tlapacoya (south-east of Mexico City) proves that by 21,000BC people were living in a region close to where the Aztecs would construct their magnificent capital city, Tenochtitlán.

EARLY INHABITANTS

For another 14,000 years, these early Mesoamericans lived as hunter-gatherers. The climate in the region was cooler than today's, and large herds of grazing animals thrived on lush grassland vegetation. Around 7000–5000BC, the settlers began to develop farming skills, gradually domesticating the plants that they had gathered in the wild. One of these in particular would become crucial to Mesoamerican civilization. A wild cereal of the region, maize, became the staple food over many centuries of selective breeding. Settlers had domesticated this grass by 5000BC.

A major climate change may have encouraged this change of lifestyle for the Mesoamerican settlers. Around 7000BC, temperatures rose worldwide and in Central America many grassland areas

Below: This Olmec stone from La Venta was probably a royal throne. The carving above the ruler's head is of a jaguar pelt.

Above: Six monoliths and 16 figures, made of jade and serpentine, were buried in this position as an offering by Olmec worshippers.

gave way either to desert or to tropical jungle. Animals were fewer and hunting became more difficult, so people turned to more intensive food cultivation.

People in the 'New World' of the Americas began to cultivate food in roughly the same era as the first farmers in the 'Old World' of the Near East and Europe, but in some ways the Mesoamericans had a harder time of it. Where the Old World farmers had cows, pigs and sheep, the peoples of Mesoamerica had only small dogs and turkeys to supplement the meat and fish they hunted. Another major difference was that the Mesoamericans had to manage without beasts of burden – they had no oxen or horses and did not even use the llamas and other camelids that were animal pack-carriers for the peoples of the central Andes who developed the Inca civilization. Partly as a result of this, Mesoamericans did not develop wheeled vehicles. Although small wheeled objects have been found in graves, it is clear that the early Mesoamericans did not have the benefit of animal-drawn vehicles or even handcarts for moving food and materials.

Over many centuries, these early farmers gradually abandoned their nomadic existence. By the time that the first Mesoamerican villages appeared, about 2000–1500BC, the farmers were raising crops of corn, chilli peppers, squashes and cotton. They were using flint knives, stone axes and very sharp cutting blades made from the volcanic rock obsidian, inhabiting thatched cane huts, weaving cloth, making pottery and fashioning evocative female figures thought to be images of an archaic fertility goddess. They appear to have lived essentially as equals in self-contained

settlements. Then, in about 1500–1200BC, the first major Mesoamerican civilization was born in the jungles of Mexico's southern Gulf coast.

THE RISE OF THE OLMEC

Labourers built awe-inspiring ceremonial centres on the banks of the region's slow-moving rivers. In the Veracruz rainforest, at San Lorenzo, men working with handbaskets raised a towering earthen platform 45m (150ft) high, topped by a cone-shaped earthen mound, by c.1200BC. At La Venta, around 50km (30 miles) downriver towards the coast, they built an earthen pyramid mound 32m (106ft) high and a ceremonial plaza in c.1000BC. The San Lorenzo complex contained the earliest stone drainage system to have been discovered in the Americas.

Craftsmen carved remarkable stone heads up to 3m (10ft) in height. These ancient works of art have characteristic flattened faces, thick lips and headgear reminiscent of a helmet. Their creation is a matter of enduring wonder. To make the carvings found at San Lorenzo, stone-cutters and labourers transported huge rocks on sledges and water-rafts over 80km (50 miles) from the Tuxtla Mountains.

The people behind these astonishing achievements lived in a more hierarchical society than their immediate ancestors. Scholars believe that the vast stone heads

Below: The priest in this Olmec carving wears a jaguar helmet. The Olmec revered the jaguar as the supreme predator.

they carved were a homage to their rulers. Great armies of labourers were needed to build their vast ceremonial centres.

This ancient culture is now called Olmec from the Aztec word for the area in which it originated. The Olmecs developed a wide-ranging trading network. At its height, their civilization had a very wide sphere of influence. Olmec-style grave objects have been found in the north-western area of Mexico City, while stone carvings exhibiting an Olmec influence were made some 1,200km (750 miles) to the south in El Salvador. However, there is no evidence that there was an Olmec empire and the civilization gradually faded in the early part of the first millennium BC. The site at San Lorenzo was destroyed in 900BC and, within 100 years, Olmec cultural and stylistic influences began to wane, although they would continue to survive for many years. The culture's full span was probably c.1500–c.400BC.

Above: Olmec sacred buildings had a major influence on those erected by their Mesoamerican descendants, such as this pyramid at the Maya site of Uaxactún.

The Olmec had lasting influence, for they bequeathed many distinctive religious ideas and practices to their descendants in the region. They developed religious rites involving human sacrifice and blood-letting, pioneered the use of ceremonial centres and invented the ball game that would remain popular right through Aztec times. They propounded the idea that the universe was divided into four directions and often carved a divine figure that combines the features of a human baby with those of a jaguar. Some scholars claim the Olmec may also have invented the writing system later developed by Mesoamerican peoples, notably the Maya. Archaeologists examining Olmec works of art have identified more than 180 symbols that may have been used as glyphs.

THE ZAPOTEC AND THE MAYA

The distinction of developing the Mesoamerican writing system is more often claimed for the Zapotec people of the Oaxaca Valley who, less than 200km (125 miles) from the centre of Olmec power, established a distinctive civilization that endured for more than 1,000 years. At the height of Olmec influence, in about 1350BC, the peoples of southern Mexico near the modern city of Oaxaca constructed a ceremonial and possibly living centre at San José Mogote. They were clearly engaged in trade with the Olmec region, for archaeologists in San José have found turtle-shell drums and conch-shell trumpets from as far north and east as the Gulf of Mexico.

DAILY LIFE

By *c.*1000BC, the settlement's central area covered almost 50 acres (20 hectares) and boasted imposing temples and tall platforms of stone. What we know of religious and daily life at San José

Below: The Zapotec were keen traders. This incense vase may have been made for sale or exchange with the people of Teotihuacán.

indicates that the city's inhabitants shared many features with the Olmec and engaged in practices that would characterize Mesoamerican culture for centuries to come. Finds of fish spines suggest that they practised blood sacrifice, for these objects are known to have been used at Maya sites for the sacred rites of autosacrifice – the letting of a person's own blood. They were also – like the Olmec – initiates of the cult of the jaguar. They made pottery that was decorated with the distinctive jaguar imagery that is associated with shamanism and Aztec worship of Tezcatlipoca. They understood the importance of measuring and marking the passage of time and, by *c.*600BC, they had begun to cut calendar symbols and early hieroglyphs at the site.

MONTE ALBÁN

Around 500BC, the peoples of the Oaxaca region built a major centre at Monte Albán. Labourers carried out vast earthworks to construct a flattened mountaintop 1km (³⁄₅ mile) in length, raising stone pyramids, temples and

Above: From early days rival Maya leaders won respect through warfare. Soldiers fought at close quarters with spears and darts.

Below: A stepped pyramid at Monte Albán gives on to a large plaza. The city has a ball court, and 170 tombs have been found there.

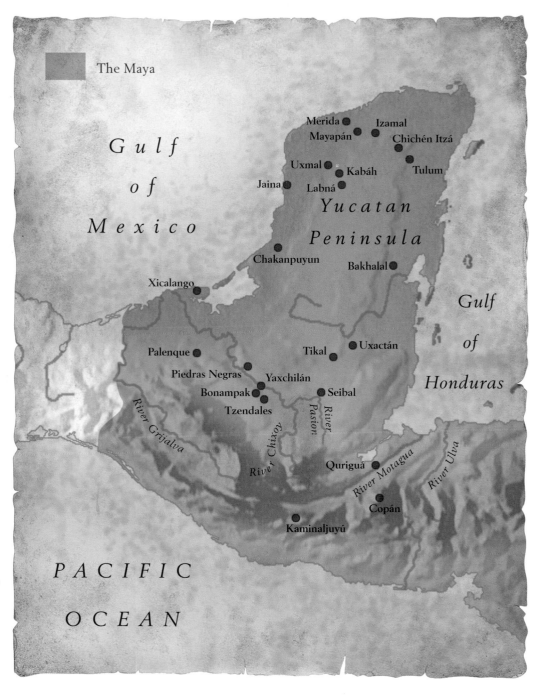

Right: In later years Maya lands stretched from Palenque in the west to Mayapán and Uxmal in the north and Copán in the east.

palaces around a vast ceremonial plaza. The site, which commands a magnificent view over the valleys below, was almost certainly built as a symbol of local power. It may have been occupied only by the political and religious elite, while the bulk of the population lived below in the valleys.

Monte Albán grew rapidly. By 200BC as many as 15,000 people lived there. Buildings spread on to painstakingly terraced lands on adjoining hills. At the height of the city's size and prestige in the period 200BC–AD200 there were 15 residential areas, each with its own plaza. Scholars do not know for sure who founded Monte Albán, but by 200BC it was occupied and controlled by the Zapotec people, who had risen to pre-eminence in the region. Monte Albán thrived as the Zapotec capital for another 1,000 years. Its people traded with the merchants of the more powerful city of Teotihuacán to the north-west.

By the 8th century AD, 25,000 people lived in Monte Albán, but in the following century the city, which had endured for more than a millennium, declined rapidly in power. The city – or its Zapotec elite – lost its hold over the people, who appear to have spread into surrounding communities.

THE MAYA

While the culture of the Olmec and Zapotec and of Teotihuacán was blooming in central Mexico, another great civilization was flowering in the jungles to the south and east, in lands that now form south-eastern and eastern Mexico, Guatemala and Belize.

Little is known of the earliest history of the Maya, partly because the tropical lands they occupied did not provide a good base in which archaeological remains could survive. But we know that village settlements with clear cultural connections to the later Maya way of life had been established by the second millennium BC on the Pacific coast of Guatemala close to the Mexican border.

Village farmers established settlements in the southern highland and central lowland regions of what were later to be the Maya homelands in the centuries after 800BC. Curiously, they do not appear to have been dominated or even influenced by the powerful Olmec culture of Mexico, perhaps because as essentially peasant villages they were not drawn into trade or cultural exchange. The Maya began to build larger ceremonial and urban settlements by c.600BC–400BC and in the four centuries after 300BC, many of the villages expanded into notable settlements as the culture thrived. A village at Tikal, in the tropical rainforest of northern Guatemala, became an important ceremonial centre. Its builders erected temples and pyramids in the years 300BC–AD100. Ceremonial buildings were also put up at Uaxactún, 20km (12 miles) to the north, before AD100. They contain giant masks that suggest a definite Olmec influence. A great city was built at El Mirador just to the north of Nakbé, with vast limestone temple pyramids on huge basalt bases.

TEOTIHUACÁN: CITY OF THE GODS

In the 1st century BC, a new power arose in the Valley of Mexico. Unknown builders laid out a magnificent city at a site 50km (30 miles) north-east of Lake Texcoco, where the Aztecs would build their capital, Tenochtitlán. The imposing ruins at Teotihuacán so overwhelmed the Aztecs that they incorporated the site into their mythology as the place where the sun and moon were created at the beginning of the current era, the 'fifth sun'. They named it Teotihuacán ('The Place of the Gods'). Historians use the name 'Teotihuacanos' for the unidentified people who built Teotihuacán.

TWO CENTRES

The inhabitants of the Valley of Mexico thrived through trade with the great Olmec civilization, exchanging highly prized local green obsidian and other goods for exotic bird feathers and sea shells. In the first millennium BC the population of the Valley grew rapidly and two centres were established, at Teotihuacán and at Cuicuilco in the south-western part of the Valley, in an area now covered by southern Mexico City.

But Cuicuilco had an unhappy destiny, for it was situated close to an active volcano. In c.100BC the volcano erupted, destroying buildings and burying the fertile agricultural lands around the city beneath rock. This natural disaster sent waves of refugees travelling north-east from the wasteland of Cuicuilco. Teotihuacán, made rich by trade in obsidian and its position on a mercantile route between the Valley of Mexico and the Gulf of Mexico, was able to take them in and the city expanded very rapidly.

PLANNED GROWTH

By AD1 Teotihuacán had upwards of 40,000 inhabitants, and it had as many as 100,000–200,000 in AD500. At this point it covered more than 20sq km (8sq miles) and was one of the largest cities in the world – far larger than the London of that era. Remarkably, its growth was not

Above: The carved head of the Plumed Serpent Quetzalcóatl adorns the pyramid built in his honour at Teotihuacán.

haphazard, for its architects followed an established layout to create a landscape of manmade foothills and mountains with a powerful symbolic meaning for Mesoamerican peoples. Scholars believe that it was built on a site of ancient

Below: The awe-inspiring Pyramid of the Moon in Teotihuacán measures 130m by 156m (426ft by 511ft) around its base.

Right: The doorway of this Maya temple at Hochob, Campeche, represents the mouth of a monster. Carvings of human figures are visible on the roof.

religious significance that may have been a place of pilgrimage long before the construction of the towering Pyramid of the Sun and Pyramid of the Moon and many centuries before the awe-inspiring Street of the Dead was laid out.

The people of Teotihuacán appear to have been cosmopolitan and to have thrived as much by trade as by war. Around two-thirds of the vast population farmed the fields that surrounded the urban development, while others worked as potters or carved tools, ornaments and weapons from the volcanic glass obsidian.

They may not have been known for their military prowess, but the Teotihuacanos engaged in religious practices that were bloodthirsty in the extreme and had a lasting effect on the rites of the Maya and Aztecs. At its height, the Teotihuacanos' influence was felt throughout Mesoamerica and left an enduring symbolic legacy in the creation of an evocative city of the divine that was to be a place of pilgrimage and worship for generations of Aztecs.

MAYA EXPANSION AND COLLAPSE

In this era, in the lands to the south and east of Teotihuacán's sphere of influence, the Maya continued to thrive. The 650 years after *c*.AD250 – the era dubbed the Classic Period by scholars – saw the Maya culture at its zenith. Important settlements were founded or expanded at Chichén Itzá, Copán, Uxmal and Palenque. At the height of the Classic Period of Maya civilization there were more than 40 Maya cities, with populations of between 5,000 and 50,000

Right: Maya cities such as Uxmal in Yucatán continued to thrive at the time of the great Maya 'collapse' in lands further south.

in each, giving a total of perhaps two million people. Most of these lived in the area known as the Maya lowlands, now in Guatemala.

Maya city-states existed in a state of almost constant conflict. Each had its ruling family and these dynasties made and broke alliances with rival rulers as the demands of conflict dictated. At the same time, Maya civilization produced a magnificent flowering of culture that produced imposing temples, pyramids

and palaces, advanced irrigation systems, a sophisticated calendar for timekeeping, elegant mathematics, detailed astronomical science and a highly developed writing system.

Around the 9th century AD, the great Maya lowland cities were suddenly abandoned. Scholars are still debating what caused this sudden change and why Maya cities situated further north in the Yucatán peninsula such as Chichén Itzá and Uxmal continued to thrive.

THE MIXTECS AND THE TOLTECS

The glory of Teotihuacán was not destined to last forever and the city's very grandeur may have contributed to its downfall. Its inhabitants laid waste to large areas of countryside to manufacture the lime needed for the mortar and stucco used in Teotihuacán's fine buildings. This may have caused erosion and reduced the amount of land available for agriculture. When food was short, a severe drought or other natural disaster may have been enough to undermine the once-unchallengeable authority of Teotihuacán's rulers. Parts of the city's complex were torched, perhaps by angry Teotihuacanos, perhaps by outsiders. At some point in the 7th or 8th centuries AD, nomads poured south into the Valley of Mexico, probably driven by changes in the climate of northern Mesoamerica that made a farmer's lifestyle unsustainable. Teotihuacán was too weak to repel them.

A POWER VACUUM

The collapse of the city, which had stood proud and pre-eminent for many centuries, created a power vacuum in which various groups competed for position. One group, the Mixtecs, rose to prominence in the Oaxaca Valley, settling and flour-ishing in the Zapotecs' former centre at Monte Albán. As well as winning a reputation for martial prowess, the Mixtecs made a name as refined craftsmen, excelling as potters, mosaic artists and goldsmiths.

THE TOLTECS

To the north-west, the Toltecs became a pre-eminent group. In about AD950 they founded the city of Tollán ('the Place of the Reeds') near modern Ṭula, about 80km (50 miles) north of the site of the later Aztec

Above: The Plumed Serpent Quetzalcóatl, a Toltec and an Aztec deity, protects this back-shield worn by a Toltec nobleman.

Below: A beautifully fashioned gold and turquoise disc bears witness to the Mixtecs' high reputation for working precious metals.

capital of Tenochtitlán. The Aztecs later viewed the Toltecs with great reverence, mythologizing them as tall, peerless warriors, ruthless conquerors, pioneers of the finest arts and sciences, developers of the Aztec calendar and year count, writers of just and lasting laws. In the Aztec account they were led in their southward expansion by Mixcóatl ('Cloud Serpent') whose son Topiltzin became identified with the god Quetzalcóatl and presided at Tollán over a city of wonderful architecture, a peaceful golden era of magnificent artistic progress, before being tricked and driven out by the warrior devotees of the war god Tezcatlipoca.

TOLLÁN

In reality, the city of Tollán was far less grand than its predecessor Teotihuacán. The exact position of Tollán was unknown for many years – indeed the Aztecs at some points identified Teotihuacán as the urban centre of the revered Toltec forebears. However, an archaeological site near Tula was identified as the remains of the Toltecs' principal city by Mexican archaeologist Jimenez Moreno in 1941. His work and further excavations have established that Tollán grew to be a centre of great importance and some size, but even at its height it was home to no more than 30,000 people, less than one-sixth of Teotihuacán's estimated population peak of some 200,000.

A MARTIAL PEOPLE

The Toltecs engaged in trade with distant regions, notably in turquoise with parts of what is now the southern USA, but they were also a martial race who, through war, expanded their territories to include the

Above: Toltec stone warriors, which stand impressively on a pyramid in Tollán (Tula), were originally painted in bright colours.

THE COLLAPSE OF TOLLÁN

A highly competitive environment lay behind the collapse of Tollán. The city of the Toltecs was destroyed in the mid- to late 12th century in the era of a ruler called Huemac, of whose depravity and failings many tales were later told. Migrations of nomads from the north had continued and the Toltecs may have met their match. The city was sacked. According to later Aztec accounts, the roof columns were torn down from Quetzalcóatl's temple, the buildings were torched and the people driven out. Many Toltecs moved on, some settling elsewhere in the Valley of Mexico, others as far to the east as the Maya city of Chichén Itzá in northern Yucatán, where architectural details such as death's-head decorations echo those in Tollán.

Following Tollán's collapse, many nomadic groups known by the name of Chichimec ('Sons of the Dog') flooded into the Valley of Mexico, competing for the most fertile territories and for strategic positions. The myth of the Toltecs' golden achievements was amplified as competing groups claimed descent from the people of Tollán. Among these peoples was a small group, the Méxica or Aztecs, who would become celebrated in history as the builders of great Tenochtitlán and rulers of a glorious empire.

bulk of the modern Mexican state of Hidalgo and the northern areas of the Valley of Mexico. Within their empire, the Toltecs settled a number of tribute areas, where garrisons kept the peace and oversaw the collection of produce; a pioneering development from which the Aztecs would learn a good deal.

Toltec culture, religious imagery and architecture celebrated ritual bloodshed and war: the capital is filled with warlike imagery. Forbidding stone columns carved in the shape of warriors stand atop one of the pyramids at Tollán and at one time held up the roof of the temple that stood there. The walls of the city's temples are decorated with soldiers wearing armour and shields on their backs and carrying spear-throwers and clumps of darts.

The temples are also adorned with gruesome *chacmools* – reclining stone figures with a bowl on the stomach in which the heart of a sacrificial victim was flung – and also contain skull racks on which heads were displayed. Scholars see in the fiercely militaristic culture of the Toltecs a reflection of a demanding political reality; a world in which tribal groups had to compete desperately for land, scarce resources and trade.

Right: Stone carvings featuring Toltec-style death's-head decorations are found in the Maya city of Chichén Itzá in Yucatán.

THE RISE OF THE AZTECS

The details of the Aztecs' origins are shrouded in myth, for this proud people told many tales that legitimized their supremacy, their use of human sacrifice and their devotion to the tribal god Huitzilopochtli. Their mytholo- gized history told how the first Aztecs or México found their origin in the island-town of Aztlán, from which they set off on a long, hazardous migration across northern landscapes, guided by Huitzilopochtli, before they came to the place on Lake Texcoco at which they were destined to found their capital, another island site identified by the divinely ordained vision of an eagle perched on a prickly cactus making a meal of a writhing serpent.

NAMING THE AZTECS

The founders of Tenochtitlán had three names in their original language, Nahuatl: Aztecs, México and Tenochcas. According to the chronicler Hernando Alvarado de

Above: A mask of Xochipilli, later worshipped by the Aztecs as the god of flowers, was found at Teotihuacán.

Tezozómoc, they were known as Aztecs because of their place of origin, the mysterious island-city of Aztlán (meaning perhaps 'White Land' or ' Land of the Cranes'), which has never been identified. The second name, México, was given to the wandering tribes by their patron god Huitzilopochtli, and scholars believe it

either comes from Méxi, one of the god's secret titles, or derives from Metzliapán ('Moon Lake'), a name for Lake Texcoco. The tribe was also called Tenochnas after Tenoch, the ruler who led it under the guidance of Huitzilopochtli in the final parts of its wandering journey. The name of their capital, Tenochtitlán, came from Tenocha while the divinely delivered appellation, the México, gave its name to the great metropolis of Mexico City that grew on that site and to the country of Mexico itself.

The founders of the empire based on Tenochtitlán called themselves 'México' and were known by this name by their Spanish conquerors. But scholars brought the name Aztec back into use in the 18th and 19th centuries and it is now the generic title for all the tribes of the Valley of Mexico in the era of the Spanish Conquest. In this book, 'México' is used where it is necessary to distinguish the people of Tenochtitlán from other tribes in the Valley of Mexico, but otherwise 'Aztec' is used to discuss the achievements and governance of the empire and the culture shared by these people.

WANDERINGS

The México wandered throughout the 12th and 13th centuries in search of a safe place to put down roots. It was a lawless time; scholars compare the southward incursions of Chichimec groups that followed the fall and collapse of Toltec civilization to the waves of barbarians that took advantage of the collapse of the western Roman empire in 5th-century Europe. A group of Chichimec – said to be led by a ruler named Xólotl, who is probably a legendary figure or a conflation of several

Left: The Toltecs cast a long shadow. Many details in the Maya city of Chichén Itzá suggest Toltec influence or conquest.

Above: The Codex Boturini, *an Aztec account of their travels, depicts ancestors leaving their original homeland, Aztlán.*

historical rulers – established themselves in the Valley of Mexico, first at Tenayuca and later at Texcoco, and formed an alliance with dispersed members of the Toltecs who were settled at Culhuacán. A group named the Tepanecs intermingled with the inhabitants of the Valley of Mexico and settled at Azcapotzalco near Lake Texcoco. The migrations of a third group, named the Acolhua, led them to eastern regions of the Valley.

The México's mythical account of their origins has it that in this period they were temporarily settled in ruins near Tula or, in some accounts, Teotihuacán. Here they learned the skills of irrigation and agriculture and developed the religious culture, including sun worship and human sacrifice, under which they later thrived. But Huitzilopochtli, diviner of the tribe's destiny, would not let them settle there and set them once more on their wanderings.

Toward the end of the 13th century, the México passed to the west of Lake Texcoco and settled at Chapultepec near some highly prized springs in a region under the control of the city of Culhuacán. The people of Azcapotzalco and Culhuacán attacked the incomers to safeguard their control of the spring waters and sacrificed the México leader. The México threw themselves on the protection of Culhuacán and were allowed to settle in the stony area of Tizapán, which was infested with poisonous snakes. Here their presence was

tolerated and they stayed for perhaps a quarter-century, using all their growing agricultural skills to raise crops in the unfriendly landscape and, according to one account, roasting the snakes to supplement their meals.

SETTLEMENT

The México intermarried with the locals and began to call themselves México-Culhua to emphasize their connection with that city's Toltec inheritance. They won honour in battle supporting the Culhua against nearby Xochimilco. However, in 1323, after a dramatic fallout with one of Culhuacán's leading nobles, they were forced to move on and to explore Lake Texcoco's marshes. Two years later, on an island around 3km (2 miles) out in the lake surrounded by marshes, they founded their new settlement, the future capital of a glorious empire that would be blessed by the bloodthirsty gods with wealth and enduring fame.

Above: The first pages of the Aztecs' Codex Boturini *detail their long migration across Mexico before founding Tenochtitlán.*

THE TWIN CITIES

Shortly after establishing Tenochtitlán, the México founded a second settlement, Tlatelolco, on another island nearby. For around 30 years, the Mexica developed their twin towns, trading with their neighbours and perfecting the science of building the *chinampa*, or artificial islands called 'floating gardens'. With careful irrigation these produced invaluable crops. The two México cities strengthened their links with the most powerful local peoples in an astute manner.

A SOCIAL CONTRACT

Tezozómoc, the brilliant Tepanec empire builder and military ruler of Azacoalco, cast a long shadow and, in the times of high tension following his death, the people of Tenochtitlán were understandably nervous about waging war against the Azcapotzalcans.

The warrior Tlacaélel delivered a declaration of war to the Azcapotzalcán leader Maxtla but, according to México accounts, the news was not well received by all at home. A public debate brought the warriors, who wished to pursue the war, into conflict with the common people, who wanted to avoid the risk of defeat. The warriors, it is said, then made a remarkable pledge in an attempt to win popular support for an attack on Maxtla. 'If we fail', they declared, 'we are yours to feast on. You will be able to slice our bodies limb from limb and eat us in your dinner pots. The war will be lost but there will be food in plenty.' This moved the people to give their agreement. 'Let it be so,' they said, 'and we will pledge that if you deliver victory in this fearful encounter we will honour you with tribute. You will be our lords. We will serve you in the sweat of our bodies and build you fine houses.'

The story legitimizes the increasing social hierarchy that accompanied changes in granting land following victory over the Azcapotzalcán leader Maxtla and the establishment of the Triple Alliance. The warriors' offer of themselves for self-sacrifice reflects the fact that it was considered an honour to be sacrificed if defeated in war and a shame to be spared or kept as a prisoner.

THE RISE OF THE AZTECS

TLATOANI 'HE WHO SPEAKS'

The chieftain at the time of the foundation of the twin cities was Tenoch. He lived for many years after 1325. He was identified as *tlatoani* ('He Who Speaks') and this was the title of the supreme ruler of the México/Aztecs until the fall of the empire. Following Tenoch's death, the México of Tenochtitlán approached the leaders of Culhuacán to ask for one of the nobles of that city, Acamapichtli, to become *tlatoani* of Tenochtitlán. There had been intermarriage between México and Culhua when the México were living near Culhualcán at Tizapán, and Acamapichtli was descended from both Culhua and México families. At the same time, the México of Tlatelolco asked for the son of a Tepanec ruler of Azcapotzalco to become their lord. Acamapichtli and the Tepanec prince were both installed as rulers with full ritual and ceremony in 1375.

A SUCCESSION OF RULERS

Under the leadership of Acamapichtli, who legitimized his rule by claiming descent from the blessed Topiltzin-Quetzalcóatl of Tollán, the México started to take a more significant part in local political events. During this period, Azcapotzalco, the Tepanec city-state, was ruled by Tezozómoc, who built up an empire through ruthless military skill and a genius for intrigue. The México people began by serving as mercenaries for Tezozómoc in his struggles against the Chichimec of Texcoco and against the Toltec of Culhualcán. In time, they built up a measure of independent power, and even expanded their territories by managing to gain *chinampa* lands in the area of Lake Xochimilco to the south of Lake Texcoco.

Acamapichtli was ruler until 1396 and he became the founder of a dynasty in Tenochtitlán,

Above: With Huitzilopochtli and Tezcatlipoca, the Plumed Serpent Quetzalcóatl was foremost among Aztec deities.

Left: An Aztec eagle carving celebrates Tenochtitlán's foundation in 1325. The Aztecs were told they would know they had found the right spot to settle when they saw an eagle on a cactus clasping a serpent.

while his younger sons and favoured followers established a ruling class in the city. He was succeeded by his son Huitzilíhuitl although, in keeping with ancient tradition, Huitzilíhuitl was elected by a council of elders rather than simply by accession to his father's place. Huitzilíhuitl strengthened the México's ties to Tepanec by marrying a grand-daughter of Tezozómoc. They continued to fight as vassals in Tepanec wars and were rewarded with grants of land, notably after wars against Xaltocán.

In the years leading up to 1426, the México made a significant advance in power and status. They fought alongside Tezozómoc against the city-state of Texcoco. The Texcocan leader Ixtlilxóchitl was forced to abandon his city and flee to the mountains, where he was killed as his young son Netzahualcóyotl looked on.

In the same year, the death of Tezozómoc further changed the balance of power in the region. Tezozómoc was succeeded, after a reign of 55 years, by his less able son Maxtla, sparking a number of conflicts between México and Tepanec that led to the assassination of Chimalpopoca, ruler of Tenochtitlán. Tensions rose to breaking point between the two cities. Maxtla prepared for war and demanded tribute from his México neighbours, while opinion was sharply divided in Tenochtitlán about the wisdom of provoking the might of Azcapotzalco.

In the end the México, now led by Itzcóatl, formed a coalition of sufficient might to let them defeat Maxtla. Netzahualcóyotl, the Texcocan prince who had witnessed the slaughter of his father was prominent in this grouping. He led a force from Huexotzingo to the southeast, where he had twice fled for his life from Tepanec attacks. Another significant coalition member was the Tepanec town of Tlacopán, which rose up and took part in the revolt against Azcapotzalco. After a siege of 114 days,

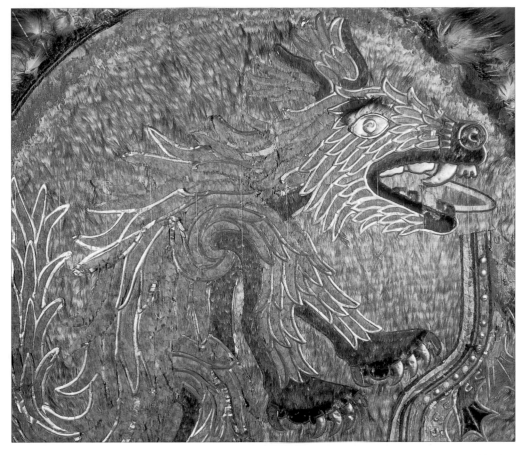

Above: The animal on this Aztec shield of c.1500 may be a coyote, a fierce creature associated with warriors and warfare.

Azcapotzalco fell and Maxtla was captured. The historian Fernando de Alva Ixtlilxóchitl reports that the defeated ruler was hauled from his place of refuge in a ritual sweat-bath and handed over to Netzahualcóyotl, who dispatched him by cutting out his heart in sacrifice.

THE TRIPLE ALLIANCE

The Tepanec empire created by Tezozómoc was no more. The three main players in the victorious coalition – Tenochtitlán, Texcoco and Tlacopán – formed a triple alliance in 1428 and divided the spoils. Tlacopán took control over land in the western region of the Valley of Mexico, Texcoco was granted much of the eastern part of the Valley, while Tenochtitlán now had power over the lands to the south and north.

This balance of power would remain essentially unchanged until the Spanish Conquest. The Aztec empire was a confederation of these three city-states, each drawing tribute from its own lands. Tenochtitlán was of prime importance: the México were the largest and most significant grouping and their capital was dominant. Next in significance was the capital of the Acolhua, Texcoco, which gained a reputation for learning, goldwork, jewellery and fine picture-manuscripts. Third, but still an enduring member of the alliance, was Tlacopán.

Below: The Plumed Serpent Quetzalcóatl was one of many gods the Aztecs inherited from their forerunners in Mesoamerica.

THE COMING OF THE SPANIARDS

Moctezuma II ruled over a great empire, but he was troubled by ill portents. In 1509, ten years before the arrival of the Spanish conquistadors, a comet appeared in the skies over Lake Texcoco. According to Friar Bernardino de Sahagún, author of *General History of the Things of New Spain*, it thrust into the sky like a tongue of flame and spilled a rain of small fiery drops as if it had broken through the canopy of the heavens. The priests and astronomers either would not or could not provide an interpretation, but the Texcocan ruler Netzahualpilli, who was believed to be able to see the future, declared that terrible events lay ahead that would usher in the destruction of the cities of the lake and of their empire. Many tales were told of unhappy omens that preceded the collapse of the Aztecs – some probably seeking with the benefit of hindsight to establish the inevitability of the Spanish triumph. Yet it appears that when the Spaniards arrived, the Aztec ruler was unsettled by doubt and ill equipped for decisive action.

REPORTS OF STRANGERS

The Aztecs must surely have known of European visitors, perhaps by word of mouth through merchants, many years before the conquistadors landed in Mexico in 1519. In 1492, the Spaniards landed in the West Indies and afterwards left their mark around the region in Hispaniola, Cuba, Venezuela and Panama. In 1502, Christopher Columbus encountered Maya traders, probably near the place now known as the Bay Islands in the Gulf of Honduras. In 1508, two Spanish sailors from Seville landed in the Maya region of Yucatán and may have inspired a drawing of what appears to be three temples borne on the sea in canoes that was seen by Moctezuma and his advisers in Tenochtitlán. Three years later, several Spanish survivors of a shipwreck off Yucatán were taken prisoner by the Maya.

In 1518, a labourer came to the imperial court reporting that he had seen mountains floating on the sea – a reference to the large Spanish ships – and Moctezuma sent advisers to the coast to investigate. They discovered reports of men with long beards and fair skin, of fishing vessels and of floating mountains.

RETURN OF THE GOD?

The most intriguing aspect of these reports was the possibility that they were portents of the return of the god Quetzalcóatl, the Plumed Serpent.

Below: Cortés and his men first explored the coast, then cut boldly inland towards Popocatépetl to find the Aztec capital.

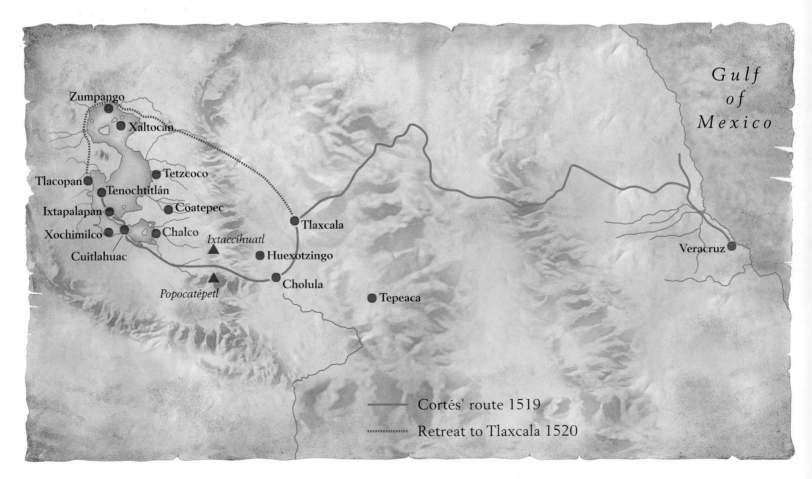

— Cortés' route 1519

⋯⋯ Retreat to Tlaxcala 1520

Above: A lookout sees the Spaniards near landfall in what Moctezuma's informers considered to be a 'floating mountain'.

According to myth, he had departed by sea heading east following the collapse of his power in Tollán and had vowed to return from that direction in order to usher in a new age. When Moctezuma was told in April 1519 that ships belonging to these sailors had made landfall in the region that would become Veracruz, it confirmed his impression, for they landed at the exact spot where Quetzalcóatl was said to have made his departure and vowed to make his second coming, and also came in the very year (1-Reed according to the Aztec reckoning) prophesied for the Plumed Serpent's return.

WELCOME VISITORS?

The Spanish expedition was led by Hernán Cortés and came from the Spanish colony in Cuba to explore the coast of Mexico. It was in fact the third exploratory Spanish trip from Cuba; the first, in 1517, had been led by Francisco Hernández de Córdoba and the second, in 1518, by Juan de Grijalva.

Moctezuma seems to have been uncertain whether to treat the incomers with reverence, as gods, or with violence, as invaders. First he sent supplies, together with magnificent offerings including large discs of gold and silver representing the sun and moon, and ritual costumes that

had been worn by performers impersonating the gods in ceremonies at Tenochtitlán. Some of the food he sent had been ceremonially doused with the blood of a sacrificial victim as was customary in the Aztec capital. Upon the rejection of his envoys by Cortés he changed his mind and dispatched sorcerers to cast spells capable of keeping the intruders in their place. However, the Spaniards proved resistant to local magic and Cortés led them inland from the coast towards the imperial capital.

He came first to the high plateau of Tlaxcala, where the locals attempted to drive the Spaniards back but were defeated. Cortés persuaded the

Tlaxcaláns, who had resisted attempts to persuade them into the Aztec empire and who were determined enemies of Tenochtitlán, to join in his campaign. The invaders came next to Cholula, which was allied to the Aztecs. As part of a plan hatched by Moctezuma, the Choluláns invited the army into the city. Hidden warriors were supposed to emerge later and put the foreigners to death. The plan was revealed to the Spaniards, however, and they slaughtered the Cholulán chiefs.

When the Spanish force and its allies came to Tenochtitlán, Moctezuma went out to meet Cortés on a palanquin carried by four noblemen and greeted the Spaniard with the utmost respect.

Below: This turquoise and shell mosaic figure formed the handle of a knife used by Aztec priests to despatch sacrificial victims.

THE COMING OF THE SPANIARDS

Moctezuma gave Cortés a necklace of snail shells and shrimps fashioned from solid gold and in return was presented with a string of Venetian glass beads. Then, in a fateful moment, he invited the Spaniards into the Aztec capital.

HOSTILITIES BEGIN

The visitors were quartered in the palace of Axayácatl near the ritual enclosure at the heart of the city. They soon saw the need to act swiftly, and were well aware that the plot that had failed in Cholula might be tried again. In an act of great simplicity and audacity, they took the Aztec emperor prisoner and kept him in guarded apartments in their palace of Axayácatl. The Aztec nobility began to prepare for violent resistance but Moctezuma urged cooperation.

Cortés had enraged the governor of Cuba by exceeding the brief of his expedition and dealing directly with Charles V in Europe. Now he was called away from Tenochtitlán to face a Spanish force sent from Cuba to arrest him. Cortés defeated the new arrivals and he persuaded the bulk of the force to return to the Aztec capital under his command. They found the city silent, but primed for explosion. In Cortés' absence, the Spaniards had attacked and slaughtered a group of Aztec nobles in order, the officers said, to put down a conspiracy.

Desperate for revenge, the Aztecs attacked the Spanish and their allies in the palace of Axayácatl. Moctezuma was persuaded to climb on to the palace roof to call for peace, but although the Aztecs obeyed their emperor, they lost their respect for him in that moment. Shortly afterward they elected Moctezuma's brother, Cuitláhuac, *tlatoani* and attacked once more. Again Moctezuma climbed to the palace parapet to calm the enraged warriors, but this time they would not hear him. They greeted his words with

Above: Moctezuma presented Cortés with a splendid quetzal feather headdress like this. Priests wore these magnificent feathers when impersonating the gods during rites.

jeers and then with a storm of arrows and stones. He was injured and later died, either from his wounds or secretly strangled by his Spanish captors, according to differing accounts.

Afterwards the Spaniards, led by Cortés, stormed the Great Pyramid itself, set fire to the shrines and threw down the Aztecs' revered idols. At every level of the pyramid the invaders were met by ferocious defenders, who hurled burning missiles down on their heads, but the well-organized Spanish force prevailed. To the people of Tenochtitlán, this defeat, and the sight of the column of smoke that rose mournfully from the ruined shrines above their once apparently invincible city, was the greatest of humiliations. In Mesoamerican warfare, the capture and sacking of an enemy temple was proof of total victory.

HASTY RETREAT

Another wave of Aztec violence was inevitable and Cortés decided to quit the city with his troops. Under cover of a moonless night and a storm of rain on 30 June 1520, Cortés' men attempted to retreat across the causeway that led westward to Tlacopán, but their movements were discovered and the Aztecs launched furious assaults on them.

Below: The ashes of Moctezuma's predecessor Ahuítzotl (1486–1502) were stored in this stone casket, which is carved with a relief of the Aztec rain god Tláloc.

Right: An illustration from Diego Durán's account of the Spanish invasion depicts Aztec warriors attacking beleagured Spaniards in Tenochtitlán.

The Spaniards and their allies lost many men in this bloody encounter. As dawn rose at the end of what was to become known as the *Noche Triste* ('Sad Night') the remnant of the Spanish army was left to lick its wounds as the Aztecs retreated, bearing booty and their partially restored honour, to Tenochtitlán.

FINAL ASSAULT

Cortés prepared for another assault on the Aztec capital. He made allies in Tlaxcala and Texcoco and a new contingent of Cholulans also joined his army. In the hour of their greatest need, the Aztecs' much-vaunted 'empire' fell apart. Even as Cortés had made his first approach to Tenochtitlán he had encountered subjects only too willing to overthrow the pride of Moctezuma.

Cortés planned to besiege the lake city of Tenochtitlán and so force its surrender. He placed armies at the head of each of the three causeways, while armed vessels or barques prevented the defending Tenochtitláns from using their usual shoreline landing places. Fighting was prolonged and bloody, but gradually the besiegers began to gain ground, pinning the defenders down in Tlatelolco. The Tlaxcaláns seized the opportunity to avenge themselves on the Aztecs with ferocious enthusiasm, piling up the bodies of their victims.

Finally, on 13 August 1521, after a siege of 93 days, the *tlatoani* Cuauhtemoc and his leading warriors were captured as they attempted to flee to a new base from which to carry on the fight. They made a dignified surrender. The Aztec empire was no more.

CONQUEST OF THE MAYA

The Spaniards found the more dispersed Maya a harder enemy to bring under control than the Aztecs.

Francisco Hernández de Córdoba, leader of the first exploratory expedition sent to Mesoamerican lands from the Spanish island of Cuba, died of wounds inflicted by Maya warriors in 1517 near what is now Champotón. The clash was the Maya's first encounter with gunpowder, but it was not their first contact with the Europeans, for Maya traders had met Christopher Columbus as early as 1502.

The second and third Spanish-Cuban voyages, led by Juan de Grijalva in 1518 and Hernán Cortés in 1518–19, largely bypassed Yucatán. It was not until 1528 that the Spaniards turned their attention to the 'northern Maya' of Yucatán. Francisco de Montejo, who led the campaign, faced a tough task. Cortés had succeeded against the Aztecs partly because he was able to isolate and undermine the authority of their emperor, but among the Maya there was no comparable figure of central authority. In addition, the pragmatic Maya fought a campaign reminiscent of modern guerrilla warfare, attacking by night and setting traps and ambushes in the difficult jungle terrain. It took the Spaniards 14 years to establish a colonial capital, at Mérida in 1542, and four years later they put resistant Maya tribes to the sword.

The southern Maya area, incorporating the Quiché and Cakchiquel kingdoms, was conquered by Pedro de Alvarado between 1523 and 1541. However, one pocket of Maya independence survived until 1697, when their lands were found to be in the path of a proposed roadway that would link Guatemala and Yucatán. When Martin de Ursua, Governor of Yucatán, sailed across Lake Flores to demand the surrender of the people of Tayasal, his ship was surrounded by Maya canoes, and when one of the Spanish soldiers fired his arquebus at the canoes it unleashed a hail of Spanish gunshot that crushed the Maya and terrified the remaining defenders into fleeing the city. The last pocket of Maya independence was defeated.

Above: Hernán Cortés moved with great directness and simplicity against the Aztecs.

CHAPTER TWO

DESERT, MOUNTAIN, LAKE AND JUNGLE

Mesoamerica was a region of great contrasts. Its landscapes range from the snowcapped volcanoes of Popocatépetl and Ixtaccíhuatl to the swampy Tabasco Plain that borders the Gulf of Campeche; from the dusty sagebrush of the northern Mexican plateau to the humid lowland jungles of El Petén in northern Guatemala.

Varied climates and landscapes called for different survival strategies. The northern Mexican plateau could only support bands of nomads; the southern part of the plateau in which lies the Valley of Mexico, was a well irrigated, fertile highland area of 800,000 hectares (2 million acres). Over many centuries, several major cultures established themselves in the Valley of Mexico, including the Teotihuacanos and the México/Aztecs. Throughout this period, warlike northern groups were a threat to their southerly neighbours and on more than one occasion they flooded southward, either to overrun local peoples or simply to settle. The México themselves came originally from the north. According to their own account of their origins, it was only after they had come south and been settled for some time near Tollán that they picked up 'civilization' in the form of the skills needed to raise crops and to irrigate the land.

Left: Tall trees and strong tropical creeper grow on the hills surrounding the ceremonial structures at the Maya city of Palenque in Chiapas, Mexico.

MANY LANDSCAPES

The variety of the Mesoamerican landscape had a significant influence on the type of civilization that developed area by area. In many parts of the region, such as the Valley of Mexico and the tropical forests of Maya lands, the peoples of Mesoamerica were blessed with fertile soil. Fed and protected by the land, they were nevertheless always at the mercy of drought and the famines it brought. The Maya and Aztecs, and their cultural predecessors, were drawn into an intense, spiritually charged relationship with the natural world. They saw the gods everywhere: in the earth, the crops that grew from it, the rain that fed the plants, the mountains where the rainclouds gathered and the wind that carried the clouds to their fields.

TOPOGRAPHY
To the east and west of the Mexican plateau rise the great mountains of the Sierra Madre Oriental and the Sierra Madre Occidental, while to its south lie the spectacular peaks of the Transverse Volcanic Axis, including Popocatépetl, Ixtaccíhuatl and Toluca. Beyond the mountains to east and west lie coastal lowlands bordering the Pacific Ocean and the Gulf of Mexico. Further south of the plateau lie more mountains, the Southern Highlands, which include the ranges of the Sierra Madre del Sur. These run down

Below: In the rainforests of Veracruz, bordering the Gulf of Mexico, the Olmec set up basalt columns to mark sacred places.

almost to the coast of the Pacific Ocean. To their east lies the lowland area of the Isthmus of Tehuantepec, beyond which the land rises to the south-east in the Sierra Madre de Chiapas and runs to the north-east into the Tabasco Plain, filled with swamps and slow-moving rivers.

MAYA LANDS
The highlands of Chiapas run eastward, linking up with the volcanic mountains in Guatemala that form the southern limit of the territories occupied by the Maya. In these uplands, where the volcanic soil is highly fertile, the Maya raised their crops with comparative ease. They also found materials that were highly valuable both for trade and their own use. These included obsidian, the hard volcanic glass used throughout Mesoamerica for the blades of knives and spears, flint and jade, the latter prized as a precious stone and often found in grave offerings. The Maya also mined basalt, which they used to make grinding stones for processing maize. In the mountain forests they

Above: In the tropical woodlands of El Petén in Guatemala, Maya cities such as Tikal and Uaxactún once defied the dense jungle.

tracked the quetzal bird, whose long green feathers were worn in costumes and headdresses by kings and priests.

To the north of the volcanic mountains, the land runs down to the lowlands of El Petén, where the first Maya settlers encountered areas of highly fertile

Below: Despite the harsh terrain of the mountainous landscape of Oaxaca's peaks, the Zapotec built a great civilization there.

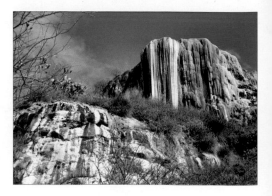

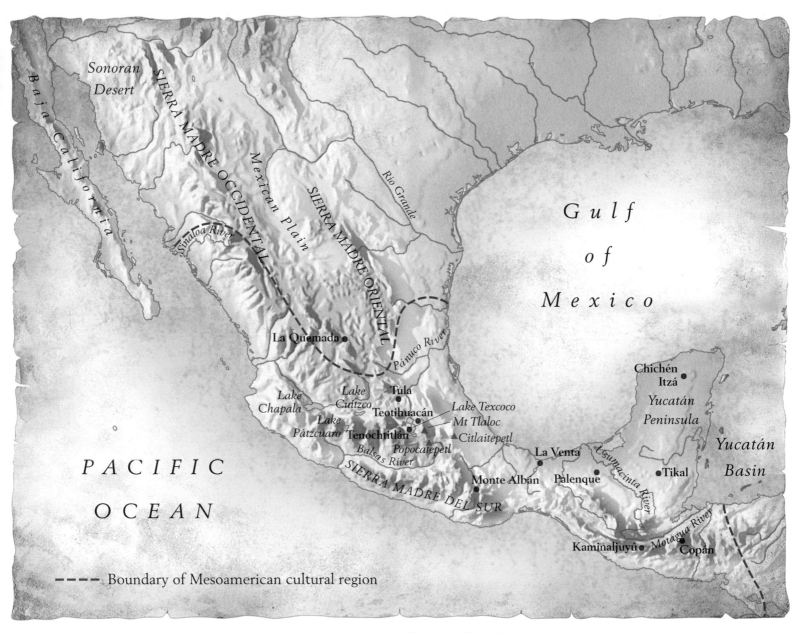

Sonoran Desert

Baja California

SIERRA MADRE OCCIDENTAL

Mexican Plain

SIERRA MADRE ORIENTAL

Río Grande

Sinaloa River

G u l f

o f

M e x i c o

La Quemada

Pánuco River

Tula

Lake Chapala

Lake Cuitzco

Lake Pátzcuaro

Teotihuacán

Tenochtitlan

Lake Texcoco

Mt Tlaloc

Citlaitepetl

Popocatepetl

Balsas River

Chíchén Itzá

Yucatán Peninsula

Yucatán Basin

La Venta

Usumacinta River

Tikal

P A C I F I C

O C E A N

SIERRA MADRE DEL SUR

Monte Albán

Palenque

Kaminaljuyú

Motagua River

Copán

- - - - - Boundary of Mesoamerican cultural region

tropical forest interspersed with low-lying seasonal swamps and areas of tall bush. In this unlikely setting they built the early ceremonial centre of Nakbé and the great cities of Calakmul, Tikal, Uaxactún and Yaxchilán. Here they felled great cedar trees that were carved into canoes 24m (80ft) in length that carried traders as far as Panama, a distance of 2,400 sea miles. They found brazil wood, which they processed as a dye for staining cloth, and collected copal, a resin exuded by tropical trees, which was burned in religious ceremonies.

Further north, Maya settlers found that the land spread out in a flat expanse covered with scrub forest, which is now known as the northern Yucatán peninsula. The name came originally from a misunderstanding, for when early

Spanish explorers from Cuba first asked the Maya what their country was called, the natives replied 'Ci-u-than' ('We cannot understand you'), which in time became 'Yucatán'. According to Bernal Díaz del Castillo, at the time of the Conquest the Maya had accepted the use of Yucatán but among themselves still called the land by its old name, which he reports was 'Land of the Deer and the Turkey'.

On the north-western edge of the lower Yucatán peninsula is a forested region known as Campeche, and to its west, bordering the Gulf of Campeche, lies the tropical area of Tabasco, filled with swamps and sluggish rivers. Here the Maya grew cacao, which was very highly prized and traded as a luxury item throughout Mesoamerica.

Above: A map of Mesoamerican terrains indicates how mountains and expanses of ocean hem in areas of very fertile land.

AREAS OF OCCUPATION

Scholars identify three areas of Maya occupation. The 'Southern Maya' were those living in the volcanic mountains of Guatemala and the highlands of Chiapas. The 'Central Maya' occupied the region stretching from Tabasco and the southern part of the Campeche through the lowlands of El Petén to Belize and part of western Honduras. This is the area largely abandoned in the 'Maya collapse' of the 9th century. The 'Northern Maya' lived in northern Campeche and towards the tip of the Yucatán peninsula. This region includes great settlements such as Chichén Itzá, Uxmal and Mayapán.

JUNGLE CITIES OF THE MAYA

We cannot know why the Maya built their cities where they did. Some are close to rivers, lakes or waterholes, but many are far from natural water sources. The lands of El Petén, which had thick tropical growth, high bush and seasonal marshes, would appear to present a daunting challenge to builders, but it was here that the first ceremonial centres and cities of the emerging Maya civilization were built. It may be that the sites were chosen by priests claiming divine inspiration; with the Aztecs and the founding mythology of their capital, Tenochtitlán, the city rose in the place that had been chosen by the gods.

Differences in farming techniques and attitudes to land between the lowlands of El Petén and the highland southern Maya regions may have had a significant impact on the types of settlement and kinds of rule that developed in the two places.

THE FARMER'S FIELD

The sacred book of the Quiché Maya, the *Popol Vuh*, tells how the sky and sea gods brought the Earth into being from the primordial waters at the dawn of time. They had only to speak the word 'Earth' and it rose up like a great mist, unfurling

Left: The great heights to which Maya builders aspired in cities such as Tikal outdid even the towering jungle trees.

and clearing to reveal the mountains and the plain. Dense vegetation spread over the terrain. The holy text likens the miraculous event to the process a Maya farmer followed to measure out a field. This was a 'four-fold siding, fourfold cornering, measuring, fourfold staking, halving the cord, stretching the cord, in the sky, on the earth, the four sides, the four corners.' Farmers across the Maya realm used a measuring technique like this, but they cleared and used the land differently in the Guatemalan highlands where the Quiché lived and the jungle-covered lowlands of El Petén, with corresponding effects on their feeling for the land and perhaps also their loyalty to their ruler.

SETTLEMENT PATTERNS

In the jungle, farmers traditionally practised 'slash and burn' agriculture. During the dry season, a farmer would use a stone axe to clear the dense growth of trees and set them ablaze. He would measure out his plot with the fourfold cornering and plant seeds of maize and other crops in the ash-enriched earth in good time for the beginning of the rainy season in May or early June. Ten years or so would usually exhaust the land on a particular plot, so after that period the farmer would move on to clear and burn another area of jungle.

In the highlands the volcanic earth was deeper and richer and farmers did not need to move their fields periodically.

Left: Shrieking monkeys were the Mayas' neighbours in the Guatemalan jungle. This pot dates from around the 9th century AD.

There, settlements were more rooted; in the jungle, farmers did not feel themselves tied to a particular piece of the land in the same way. Scholars believe that this contributed to the long-term instability of the jungle city-states. The cities were close together, often no more than a day's march apart. As farmers moved further away from the stone towers of their own settlement, they may have felt increasingly vulnerable to interference or attack.

Kings commanded loyalty by military ability, charisma and their capacity to demonstrate power through great public sacrificial rituals on the temple-pyramids of their ancestors. This type of loyalty could quickly melt away if a king was defeated, captured and sacrificed – and the next member of his dynasty was weak. The result was that a succession of kingdoms rose to brief pre-eminence, then were conquered or faded away.

INTENSE COMPETITION

Recent archaeological work has transformed our idea of what the jungle and the jungle cities would have looked like in the 8th or 9th centuries AD. At one

time, scholars thought that the Maya of the lowland jungles were relatively few in number and that there was plenty of land for clearance and sowing. But the latest evidence indicates that in the 8th century the Maya population in the jungle lowlands was extremely high and that the Maya at this time were farming the land intensively. We now know the Maya jungle farmers cleared slopes and built terraced fields and even constructed raised fields in the region's low-lying swamps.

It appears that by the 8th century the Maya had cleared the jungle almost completely. The lush vegetation that now almost swamps many of the jungle cities is secondary rather than primary growth. Modern tourists climb the towering

Below: In the mid-20th century the lush forest of El Petén swamped Tikal. Clearing work, beginning in 1956, uncovered the city.

pyramids of sites such as Tikal and look down beyond the city limits on the tall green towers of the forest, but a Maya priest in the same position in the 8th century would have looked down on land that had been cleared and set aside for farming.

Many scholars now believe that this state of affairs holds the key to the 'Maya collapse' – the abandonment of the cities of the region in the 9th century that

Above: The temples of Palenque stand on the densely forested foothills of the Sierra Madre, overlooking the plain of Chiapas.

marks the end of the Classic Period. They argue that the overuse of the land caused an ecological catastrophe. There was no longer enough land to go round and what territory there was was not highly fertile. The Maya city-states fought bitterly over the last available areas of good land.

SACRED MOUNTAINS IN THE JUNGLE

Mountains were revered throughout Mesoamerica. To the Maya, they were the place where deceased ancestors lived on and even today the Maya peoples of the Chiapas region hold to this belief. The architects of the El Petén region and northern Yucatán lived many miles north of the Chiapas highlands and the volcanic mountains of southern Guatemala, but in cities such as Tikal, Palenque and Uxmal they created their own sacred mountains in the form of the stepped stone pyramids that today still tower above great ceremonial plazas.

THE PYRAMIDS

Pyramids were identified by the word *witz*, which could also mean 'mountain'. A pyramid was a sacred building with a temple at its summit, used for ceremonial processions and religious rituals. However, they were also, and perhaps primarily, mortuary monuments, erected to honour the memory of a dead king. Both

Below: The ceremonial centre at Uxmal, in Yucatán, is bounded to the right by the soaring Pyramid of the Magician.

symbolically (as a stone mountain) and literally (as a giant tomb) they were homes to deified royal ancestors.

It may be that the temples on top of the pyramids were architectural versions of the natural caves in which Mesoamericans had left offerings from time immemorial. Some – such as those

Above: Access to the Temple of the Masks, Tikal, at the top of the staircase and halfway to heaven, was restricted to the priesthood.

at Tikal and Yaxchilán, for example – had large vertical roofcombs that reinforced the impression that they were openings in a rockface close to the sacred sky. Many of the pyramids, like mountains, presented a forbidding challenge to those seeking to climb them. They towered to great heights, their stepped sides were very steep and the steps themselves so narrow that the members of the religious procession mounting to the holy places on high would have had to put their feet sideways on each step.

SACRED STRUCTURES

Other architectural elements of the Maya city were representations in stone of the sacred structures of the universe and of the natural world around them. In Maya culture, water was linked to the underworld; a number of surviving carvings represent royal passengers in a canoe on their final voyage to the spirit world. Scholars believe the great ceremonial plazas of Maya cities represented lakes or

suggest the nine regions of the underworld the king encounters as his soul makes its voyage through the spirit realm. One construction at Tikal, Temple II, has three layers. At Izapa, in the Pacific coastal region of Chiapas, a plaza contains three pillars, each 1.3m (4ft 3in) tall and supporting a circular stone. Both the Tikal temple and Izapa pillars are symbolic references to the three hearthstones of the Maya creation myth, which the Maya believed were visible in the night sky as the three stars in Orion's belt.

In man-made versions of natural holy places, the gods could be honoured with sacrifices designed to recycle spiritual and cosmic energy (largely in the form of life-blood) on behalf of the city state. Maya kings, priests and people hoped that the sacrifices would safeguard the flow of divine power needed to keep the natural world functioning; the sun rising, the rain clouds forming and unloading their cargo, the land giving birth to maize plants.

Below: At Cobá, in Quintana Roo, a rounded pyramid rises like a natural mountain peak from the jungle floor.

Above: The steep incline of the steps – as here at Palenque – made it a demanding task to climb to the holy places above.

seas that offered a way to the underworld. Some scholars believe the Maya thought the ball court, specifically, represented an entry to the underworld, while the ball used in the game represented the sun. Even the stone columns or stelae on which rulers recorded their dates of accession, anniversaries of their rule and political or military triumphs were associated with the natural world. The Maya word for the stela was *te tun* ('tree rock'). The stelae at Yaxchilán, for example, rise toward the sacred sky in the same way as the trees of the forest in which the city stands.

UNDERWORLDS AND HEARTHSTONES
The structures of pyramids, temples and plazas had detailed religious and mythic significance. For example, temples at Palenque and Tikal with nine levels

WATER: A SCARCE RESOURCE

Because of the physical characteristics of their lands, the Maya often had to come up with ingenious solutions to provide water for their cities and their people.

Below: Some cenotes *or underground waterholes, such as this well at Dzitnup, are accessible only through a small opening.*

FRESH WATER

In the northern part of the Yucatán peninsula there are no large rivers and early in the dry season, which can last six months, all streams disappear. The land is porous limestone; water runs through the rock and collects below ground. In places, the land has collapsed, forming

Above: The city of Tulum on the cliffs of eastern Yucatán is battered by ocean winds and washed by Caribbean spray.

vast holes – some 60m (200ft across) and 30m (100ft) deep – which are fed by underground rivers. These holes, called *cenotes*, are used as wells.

CENOTES

Chichén Itzá was built around two *cenotes*. The earliest settlers constructed the city in the 5th century around the southernmost of the two wells. They built two stairways of masonry 20m (65ft) down to the water. The city was 'refounded' by the Itzá in the years after AD987, based on a second *cenote* further north. This second well is around 60m (200ft) across, while its rim is 22m (73ft) above the surface of the water. While they continued to use the southern *cenote* for drawing water, they used the northern one for religious rituals. A sacred causeway 275m (900ft) in length runs from the Great Plaza northward to the 'Well of Sacrifice'.

According to Bishop de Landa, the Maya held sacrifices to the rain god Chac during droughts, in which priests threw

Right: With two wells, Chichén Itzá had a plentiful water supply. This is the northern waterhole, set aside for religious rites.

human victims into the well with offerings of precious gold and jade. De Landa suggests that the Maya did not think that the victims died, although they did not see them again once they had been cast into the well. A colourful 19th-century addition to the folklore surrounding the sacred well suggested that beautiful virgins were cast into its water to please Chac. Edward Thompson, US Consul to Merida, bought the site of Chichén Itzá in 1901 and had the well dredged, turning up precious offerings and the remains of human sacrifices. Biological anthropologist Ernest Hooton examined skulls found in the well and found them to include skulls of men, women and children.

Another celebrated *cenote* existed at Bolonchen ('Nine Wells') in the Campeche, where water lies 135m (450ft) below the surface. The American traveller and archaeologist John Lloyd Stephens, author of *Incidents of Travel in Central America, Chiapas, and Yucatán* (1841), visited the site and described how, by the light of pine torches, the Maya descended over crumbling rock deep into the earth using a long ladder made from

Below: At Labná, near Uxmal in the Puuc region of Yucatán, rainwater was collected in a specially constructed cistern.

great planks of wood lashed together, with earthen pots for carrying the water tied to their backs and heads. His companion Frederick Catherwood made a celebrated lithograph of the Bolonchen well in use, showing heavily laden natives clambering down to the water and up to the light.

RESERVOIRS AND RIVERS
In some places the Maya made their own reservoirs. The city of Tikal had no access to water from springs, rivers or wells but rainfall was plentiful. Its inhabitants relied on the water collected in a great reservoir situated just off the city's ceremonial centre. Its builders lined two natural ravines with clay and left them to dry in the sun, thus creating a water-tight area. They added a causeway across the reservoir that also functioned as a dam. Rainwater could flow in freely from the ceremonial area: the builders laid the plaza so that its surface tilted at an angle of five degrees from level to encourage water-flow into the reservoir. The Maya also built wells that collected rainwater as it ran off the roofs of houses and ceremonial buildings. The wells had their own roofs to limit evaporation of the precious liquid during hot weather.

Some Maya cities were built within convenient reach of water. Yaxchilán and Piedras Negras, for example, were built alongside the River Usumacinta. At Palenque, which lies just above the floodplain of the Usumacinta, the River Otulum runs right through the site: here the builders diverted the river into an artificial waterway that passes beneath the palace. Cobá, in north-eastern Yucatán, was situated between two lakes.

SALT WATER
Some Maya cities were built on the coast, facing the ocean. The builders of Tulum erected their city atop a 12m (40ft) limestone cliff on the coast of eastern Yucatán looking down on the Caribbean Sea. Built in the 6th century AD, it was still occupied by the Maya at the time of the Conquest. The city's name means 'fence' or 'wall' and came into use after the arrival of Europeans because Tulum is enclosed on its inland sides by high walls. Its ancient name may have been Zama ('dawn') because it faces east to greet the jaguar sun god each morning on his emergence from the underworld.

Tulum greatly impressed Europeans when they first encountered it. The 1518 Spanish exploratory mission led by Juan de Grijalva sailed down the coast and Juan Díaz, the mission chaplain, reported he had seen three great towns, one as large as Seville with a great tower. Tulum contains a tall building known as El Castillo ('the castle'), with a temple on its top. The city was connected by a stone causeway which led to Xelha and to Chichén Itzá.

CITY OF AWE: TEOTIHUACÁN

The impressive setting, the towering architecture and the vast grid layout of Teotihuacán struck awe into Aztec hearts. They knew nothing of the historically distant peoples who erected this symbolic urban landscape and became convinced that its architects must have been the gods themselves.

CITY OF THE GODS
Teotihuacán lies in a side valley running off the Valley of Mexico, around 50km (30 miles) north-east of the Aztec capital Tenochtitlán. Its unknown founders may have chosen the setting because of its proximity to a rich source of the highly prized volcanic glass obsidian and to the San Juan river, which provided water for agriculture. The site also lay on a significant trade route that ran to the Gulf Coast from the Valley of Mexico.

The Aztecs were deeply impressed by the architecture and stylized grid pattern of Teotihuacán. Their powerful mythological imagination saw in the Pyramids of the Sun and Moon the setting for the divine rituals that set the modern

Above: Goggle eyes and fanged mouth identify this Teotihuacán carving as the rain god. The Aztecs worshipped him as Tláloc.

era in motion and raised the life-giving sun and his pale companion the moon in the skies. However, to the Aztecs who made pilgrimages to the site to gaze in awe at the vast buildings, to make sacrifices and offerings to the gods, to consult oracles and to put criminals to a bloody death, this city of man-made mountains laid out against a backdrop of natural peaks was

a deeply moving statement of religious devotion and its power to safeguard a world that could at any moment be brought to an abrupt end by the gods.

SITE OF ANCIENT PILGRIMAGE
As well as being the imagined setting for primal mythological events, Teotihuacán had other deeply seated religious and spiritual associations. At some points in their history, the Aztecs identified Teotihuacán with the revered civilization of Tollán, whose golden age of fertile lands, divine leaders and just laws represented an earthly paradise. The Aztecs believed that the people of Tollán had flourished in the era immediately before their own rise in the 14th century, and so imagined the flowering of Teotihuacán to have taken place more than 500 years after the city's actual primacy (c.100BC–AD650).

Moreover, the great Pyramid of the Sun was erected atop a natural cave that was a site of ancient religious observance. The cave, discovered during architectural investigations in 1971, contains remains of religious offerings made many centuries before the pyramid was raised in honour of the gods in around AD150. From time immemorial, Mesoamerican peoples saw caves as gateways to the world of spirit; scholars suggest that these offerings may have been part of rituals that were based on archaic shamanistic practice and that the cave and surrounding area may long have been an area visited by the devout. This holy site was the natural spot for the construction of the Pyramid of the Sun, the most sacred of the buildings in Teotihuacán.

SACRED LANDSCAPE
The Pyramid of the Sun stands 66m (216ft) high, a great man-made mountain containing 765 million cubic metres

Left: Priests standing atop the Pyramid of the Moon would have been able to look directly down the 'Street of the Dead'.

Above: Teotihuacán made an evocative setting for Aztec religious rites. The moon hangs above the wide 'Street of the Dead'.

(1,000 cubic yards) of laboriously quarried rock that dominates the centre of the city. It stands to the east of the ceremonial roadway that was dubbed the 'Street of the Dead' by the Aztecs. This roadway, 40m (130ft) wide, runs for 2.4km (1.5 miles) and lies 16 degrees to the east of true north, so that it runs exactly towards Cerro Gordo, an extinct volcano revered as a sacred mountain. The road, which forms the basis of the city's grid pattern, is lined with lower buildings that the Aztecs believed were the tombs of ancient kings, but which are now known to have been palace residences. At the northern end of the road, situated so that it is framed by Cerro Gordo, stands the city's second largest construction, the Pyramid of the Moon, 43m (140ft) tall. The pyramid's main stairway gives directly on to the Street of the Dead. The Pyramid of the Sun and the Pyramid of the Moon probably had temples on their flattened tops.

The southern part of the Street of the Dead gives to the east on to a 15-hectare (38-acre) sunken square courtyard called the Citadel, which contains the temple of Quetzalcóatl, a stepped pyramid-platform whose decorated walls bear numerous stone sculptures representing Quetzalcóatl and Tláloc. Many burials have been found near the temple, including a ceremonial interment dated to AD200 of 18 men, probably captured soldiers put to sacrificial death.

The vast city of Teotihuacán amazes even the modern visitor with its grandeur and scale. The city contained 2,000 apartment buildings, 600 pyramids and many other temples, plazas, administrative buildings and palaces used by nobles and priests. There were 500 areas of workshops where craftsmen made pots or worked in obsidian and a vast marketplace served by merchants from many parts of central America. Its construction must have been the work of generations

of Teotihuacanos and is an astonishing, enduring proclamation of the power of the city's rulers. The city's great stone peaks honour and echo the natural mountains that range against the sky behind them. It is not difficult to understand the Aztecs' reverence for its architects.

Right: Heads of Quetzalcóatl flank the steep stairs of a Teotihuacán temple. One of the god's aspects was as the wind deity Éhecatl.

'WATER MOUNTAIN': TENOCHTITLÁN

The Spanish conquistadors encountered Tenochtitlán at the height of its glory, a vast metropolis on the water with more than 150,000 and perhaps as many as 300,000 inhabitants. They were moved to compare it to the Italian city of canals, Venice, or even to the enchanted cities described so colourfully in medieval chivalric romances. Yet the Aztecs constructed what appeared to be a city of dreams from the most unlikely of beginnings.

FOUNDING OF A CITY

The México/Aztec incomers who founded Tenochtitlán were latecomers in the Chichimec incursions that followed the collapse of Toltec power in the 12th century. When they arrived in the Valley of Mexico in the mid-13th century, the best territories had already been settled and the México were not made welcome by the Alcohua, Tepanec and other groups who had already made their homes there. Moreover, the newcomers were driven out of the places where they did settle. When they finally brought their wanderings to an end in 1325, the México

had to take what lands they could get. The twin islands on which they were to found their great city were some of the least attractive lands in the vicinity, so unpromising that none of the three powers in the region of Lake Texcoco – Texcoco to the east, Azcapotzalco to the west and Culhuacán to the south – had bothered to lay claim to them.

The city had to be designed to fit the setting and its island situation and marshy surroundings were crucial shaping factors from the start. Certainly there were some benefits to the site. For food, the settlers had their pick of the fish, birds and plentiful waterlife. Indeed, the Aztecs came to view the lake as a mother who had given them refuge at her breast. In fertility rites held on the lake each year, the water was addressed as Tonanueyatl ('Mother Vast Water'). The watery setting was also an advantage in terms of transport. In a country where men and

Left: 'Floating fields' such as these created in Lake Xochimilco were needed to support the burgeoning population of Tenochtitlán.

Above: The Aztecs' reliance on causeway or boat to connect to the lake's shore is clear in this schematic image of Tenochtitlán.

women made no use of beasts of burden or wheeled carts, it was easier to move things by canoe. The islands were also in a central position, within a triangle formed by the lake's three foremost cities. This was important strategically and was also of benefit to the México when they established marketplaces in Tenochtitlán and Tlatelolco.

LAYOUT AND DESIGN

The Aztecs laid their city out in four quarters to match the four cardinal directions and built a sacred precinct at its centre. Each of the *capultin* or tribal clans was assigned its own area and its own temple within the city; the clans held their land communally. The Great Pyramid and ritual precincts that developed here were understood by the Aztecs to be the centre of the universe. The pyramid itself was a holy mountain, a reproduction within the city of

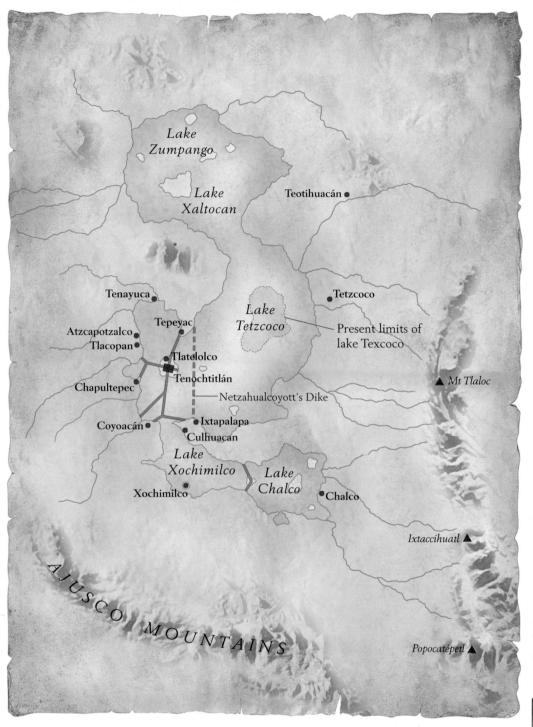

in pairs with a central footpath and canals on either side from which the farmers could draw water to irrigate the crops. Canoes used the canals to transport goods. *Chinampa* varied in size from 100sq m to 850sq m (1,100 to 9,000 sq ft). A typical *chinampa* might be farmed by 10–15 people. The available land was greatly increased after the Aztec under Itzcóatl took control in 1428 of the large *chinampa* plantations in the freshwater lakes of Xochimilco and Chalco that lay to the south of Lake Texcoco.

The city's location and design made it vulnerable. It could easily be flooded. A flood in 1500 destroyed many houses. Netzahualpilli, son of Netzahualcóyotl of Texcoco, told the Aztec *tlatoani* Ahuítzotl that the gods must be enraged. A great reconstruction project was launched: the nobles built palaces, dykes were strengthened and willows and poplars planted along the canals. The second, ultimately disastrous, drawback was that the city was not self-sufficient and could be cut off, making it vulnerable to siege. Sadly for the Aztecs, Hernán Cortés saw this. He blocked the three causeways and used a fleet of armed barges to prevent food being brought in any other way. The three-month siege led to the city's fall and the end of the Aztec empire.

Above: Netzahualcóyotl built a 16-km- (10-mile) dyke to seal off the freshwater part of the lake containing Tenochtitlán.

the sacred heights of Popocatépetl, Ixtaccíhuatl and Mount Tláloc. The city itself was a mountain on the lake – indeed the Nahuatl word for 'city', *atl tepetl*, translates as 'water mountain'. They built three long causeways, said by Hernán Cortés to be 3.5m (12ft) wide, to link the islands to the mainland. An aqueduct carried water in from mainland springs at Chapultepec hill.

CHINAMPA

Agricultural land was initially in short supply until the Aztecs developed their own *chinampa* or 'floating fields'. In shallow water, these fields were built up in the lake bed with layers of mud and plants, fixed in place by tall posts. In deeper water, fields were made by filling 'floating' reed-beds with earth and anchoring them to the lake bed. The plots were laid out

Right: An illustration from the manuscript of the Codex Mendoza *(c.1541) represents Tenochtitlán as a city founded on water.*

ON THE EDGE: COPÁN AND JAINA ISLAND

The city of Copán, which lay close to the Guatemala–Honduras border, was the most easterly of the large Maya cities. For the Maya, Copán lay at the eastern limits of their civilization.

The site at Copán was occupied from 1000BC onwards, but for many centuries it was only a small farming settlement. Copán developed into a major city c.AD400, when a group of public buildings and a ball court were erected.

OPENING TO THE UNDERWORLD

By the 9th century, the city had as many as 20,000 inhabitants. It covered 100 hectares (250 acres) and contained two large pyramids, as well as several plazas, stairways and stone temples, most arranged on a central raised platform called the Acropolis by archaeologists. In the 7th century, King Smoke Imix made the city a leading power in the world of the Maya.

Through architecture, the king also sanctified Copán: the arrangement of his

Above: These figures on Altar Q at Copán represent Yax Pak (centre) receiving a sceptre from his ancestor Yax K'uk Mo'.

stelae in the city and the valley around it identify the place as a sacred opening to the underworld. His descendant Smoke Shell built a magnificent dynastic stairway 15m (50ft) wide and with 1,250 hieroglyphs on the risers of its 72 steps, from which scholars have been able to trace a dynasty of 16 kings who ruled the city from Yax K'uk Mo' ('Blue Quetzal Macaw') in c.AD435 to Yax Pak ('First Sunrise') in AD820.

For many years, scholars believed that the city had a special significance for Maya civilization as a centre for study of astronomy and astrology. There is no doubt that astronomy fed strongly into the city's development. Many of the buildings and stelae erected in the reign of the 9th-century monarch King 18 Rabbit are arranged to mirror the sacred patternings of the sky. The stelae bear many detailed carvings of the king. One shows him as both a young man and an

Left: King 18 Rabbit, subject of several stelae at Copán, oversaw a major building programme in the city in the early AD700s.

older king, while another depicts him wearing both the jaguar-skin garment associated with kings and a beaded dress of the kind usually seen in depictions of women. As Maya scholar John S. Henderson has noted, the images, their positioning and the hieroglyphic inscriptions suggest a number of highly significant symbolic oppositions, including left–right, young–old and female–male – as well as the three realms sky–world–underworld and the four directions east–north–west–south.

ALTAR Q

Much of the scholarly debate about the significance of Copán was generated by misinterpretation of a square structure with 16 figures carved on its sides. The object, called Altar Q by archaeologists, was built by King Yax Pak in the 9th century. Historians used to believe that the figures on the altar were those of

Above: A stela honouring King Smoke Imix, 12th ruler in Yax K'uk Mo's dynasty, overlooks part of the ball court at Copán.

Below: This figurine from Jaina Island wears a fine cotton blouse, suggesting that she is a woman of high rank.

astronomers called to Copán to adjust the Maya calendar. We now know that the individuals are Yax Pak and his 15 ancestors in the dynasty of Yax K'uk Mo'. Copán might have been at the limit of Maya realms, but it had dynastic links with other Maya cities. Scholars believe that the dynasty descended from Yax K'uk Mo' had connections among the royal family at Tikal – the Copán emblem glyph has been found in texts at Tikal. The mother of the dynasty's final king, Yax Pak, was from Palenque.

At the other end of the Maya realm lay the enigmatic Jaina, a limestone island off the coast of Campeche that the Maya used as a burial ground in the late Classic Period (during the 7th–9th centuries AD) and where archaeologists have found a wealth of small clay figurines in graves. The island's westerly location made it a natural choice for a cemetery. Viewed from the mainland, the sun would have set behind Jaina on its nightly journey to the spirit realm. Its setting in the ocean also made it appropriate, for lakes, seas and expanses of water were considered to offer a passage to Xibalba. The clay figures represent women and men of different social levels and may be portraits of the deceased. Some of them certainly depict deities, notably the sun and moon gods, who in mythology survived the frightful realm of the underworld to rise immortal into the sky.

THE JEWEL OF THE CEREN

To the south of Copán lies a farming village that was of little importance in Maya times, but which is of great interest to archaeologists because a volcanic eruption in c.AD590 buried its buildings in ash, so preserving them in perfect condition for future generations to explore and analyse.

The village, now known as Joya del Ceren ('Jewel of the Ceren'), was discovered in 1976 by the American anthropology professor Payson D. Sheets. It appears that the inhabitants of the village were able to flee the disaster, but they left behind a treasure trove of tools, materials, household furniture and even food, enabling Professor Sheets and other scholars to build up a convincing picture of life in a Maya farming village during the Classic Period. Surviving structures include adobe houses, public and religious buildings and a communal bathhouse.

CHAPTER THREE

APPEASING THE GODS

In 1428, Maxtla, ruler of the once-dominant Tepanec city of Azcapotzalco, was decisively defeated by a coalition of Tenochtitlán, Texcoco and Tlacopán. He was taken prisoner and put to ritual death in a ceremony that is revealing of the many ways in which war and blood sacrifice served to legitimize political power and safeguard the natural order in Mesoamerica.

The ceremony was a graphic demonstration of the triumph of the new Triple Alliance of Tenochtitlán, Texcoco and Tlacopán at the expense of the waning Tepanec empire. Maxtla's sacrifice was also a symbolic appropriation of Tepanec lands into the domain of the Triple Alliance and an expression of Netzahualcóyotl's primacy in his own city-state; he would become ruler of Texcoco three years later. However, the sacrifice had a number of more general, and more significant, symbolic meanings. First was its link to fertility. Netzahualcóyotl and all those present trusted that the offering of the victim's lifeblood would safeguard the richness of the soils, guarantee the return of the rains and therefore promote a good harvest. Second, the ritual was a renewal of the state itself, validating the power of the ruler and the war that was his weapon, keeping chaos and dissolution at bay. Third, the killing of Maxtla was an act of respect, for Mesoamericans considered it shameful for a warrior or ruler to be captured and kept alive and believed it was an honourable fate to be despatched as a human sacrifice.

Left: In sacrificial rites, the victim's heart was flung into the container on the flat belly of a chacmool *figure. This* chacmool *reclines outside the Temple of the Warriors in Chichén Itzá.*

MANY TYPES OF BLOOD OFFERING

For Mesoamerican peoples, offering human blood in sacrifice was a religious duty, necessary to sustain the world by maintaining the fertility of the land and the power of the ruler. It was also vital for satisfying the gods, who might at any moment determine to bring the present age to a violent end. Humans, gods and the natural world were part of a cosmic pattern of energy in which ritual and sacrifice were the means by which energy was recycled or passed on. Among the Aztecs, the two most common forms of sacrifice were extracting the victim's heart from his chest and burning to death.

REMOVING THE HEART

The extraction of the heart was performed with great ceremony on a special sacrificial block known as a *quauhxicalli* ('Stone of the Eagle'). The stone was pointed in the centre, so that a victim thrown down on it would be forced to arch his back and so thrust up his chest ready for the sacrificial knife.

Post-Conquest Spanish accounts report that naked victims were grouped at the foot of the temple steps as a priest descended from the sacred heights of the temple with an image of the god in whose honour the sacrifice was to be made. He showed the divinity to each victim, saying, 'this is your god', before the victims were led up to the sacrificial stone. Six priests of the highest rank (*chachalmua*) performed each sacrifice: four to hold the victim's feet, one to hold his throat and one to cut his chest. The foremost of these priests, dressed in a splendid red tunic and his head adorned with a helmet of yellow and green feathers, sliced the victim's chest with a flint knife known as a *técpatl*. He tore the heart from the chest, held it up to the sun, then cast it steaming before the image of the god. The six priests together pushed the corpse off the sacrificial stone and down the bloodstained temple steps. Bodies gathered at the foot of the steps in a bloody pile. Later on, they were collected, prepared and eaten in a respectful and devout ritual.

BURNING

Sacrifice by burning was mainly reserved for ceremonies in honour of the fire god Xiuhtecuhtli, who was sometimes worshipped as Huehuetéotl ('The Old

Above: In a carved lintel at Yaxchilán, King Shield Jaguar's wife Lady Xoc draws a blood offering from her tongue.

God'). The rite represented the rebirth of the god, the rising of new life from death in the same way the sun was born when the god Nanahuatzin cast himself into the flames in an act of divine self-sacrifice. Other sacrificial methods were similarly

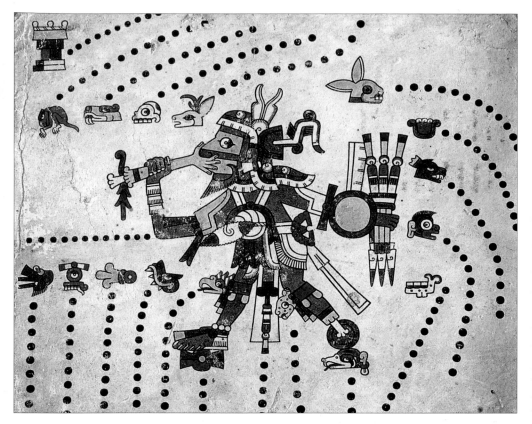

Above: A 16th-century codex illustration depicts Tezcatlipoca, dark lord of fate, feasting on the body of a sacrificed prisoner.

associated with particular gods. Victims killed in honour of Xipe Totec, the god of planting and vegetation, were shot with arrows so that their blood flowed into the earth like life-giving waters. Indeed, the Aztecs called human blood *chalchiuatl* ('precious water'). The corpse was then flayed and a priest would wear the skin in honour of the god, who was known as 'Our Lord the Flayed One'. The rite was a celebration of the splitting of seeds that makes possible the growth of new vegetation each spring.

MAYA METHODS

The Maya also used the primary Aztec method of slicing the victim's chest and extracting his dripping heart to offer to the gods. The priest oversaw the rite. Four aged men, called *chacs* in honour of the Maya rain god, were positioned to hold the body of the victim on the sacrificial stone while a specialist named the *nacom* cut open the victim's chest. In the Classic Period, however, many Maya sacrificers preferred to decapitate their victims. They also cast victims into the waters of their sacred wells or *cenotes* to drown. The American archaeologist Edward H. Thompson found the skeletons of many men, women and children in the *cenote* at Chichén Itzá.

Autosacrifice or offering one's own blood to the gods was practised. The Maya used a string threaded with thorns to cut their cheeks, lower lips, ears and tongues. They collected blood and then smeared it on images of the god or on their own body or hair. Men also used sharp knives or the spines of stingrays to cut and draw blood from their penises for offering in the same way. Among the Maya, ritual bloodletting of this kind was considered a privilege and was performed by members of the nobility. At important times, such as the passing from one calendrical cycle to another, the king and his family would perform the ritual in honour of his ancestors and on behalf of himself, the city-state and his people. There are also illustrations in Maya codices, on door lintels and on ceramics, of the gods themselves letting their blood in this way. A vase unearthed at Cahal Pech near Belize depicts a figure with the appearance of the sun god drawing blood from his penis.

Among the Aztecs, the offering of one's own blood was the preserve of priests. They would perform the rite prior to important state events and at auspicious and inauspicious dates in the calendar. They used maguey spines or blades of the volcanic glass obsidian to cut their earlobes and prick their legs and arms, or would run a thorned cord across their tongue or penis. In the rites prior to investiture as *tlatoani*, the new ruler would offer his own blood – drawn in this way from his earlobes, calves or arms – before the shrine of Huitzilopochtli atop the Great Temple in Tenochtitlán.

Animal sacrifices were also made. The Aztecs slaughtered many quails, ripping their heads off before images of the gods. Quails were associated with the myth of Quetzalcóatl, in which the Plumed Serpent descended to the underworld at the end of the previous age of the world, in order to take the bones of a previous race of men and use them to create a new tribe of humans to inhabit the current age. The underworld god Mictlantecuhtli was angry and ordered quails to chase him. Both Aztecs and Maya also sacrificed turkeys, dogs and, on special religious or state events, jaguars. In the Maya city-state of Copán, 16 jaguars were killed to mark the accession of the 16th king, Yax Pak. The bones of a jaguar were also placed among the foundations of the Great Temple in Tenochtitlán.

Left: An elaborate knife such as this was used to dispatch sacrificial victims. The handle of this weapon represents a warrior.

49

MESOAMERICAN DIVINITIES

CREATORS

AZTEC

Ometecuhtli, dual nature male and female as Ometeotl and Omecihuatl. Also took form of Tonacatecuhtli and Tonacacihuatl.
Tezcatlipoca, sometimes seen as supreme creator god.

MAYA

Itzamná, also known as Hunab Ku. In *Popol Vuh* Huracán (Hurricane or Sky Heart, sky god creator) and Gucumatz or Kukulcán (Sovereign Plumed Serpent, sea god creator). Kukulcán is the Maya equivalent of the Aztec god Quetzalcóatl.

Tezcatlipoca   *Itzamna*

SUN, MOON AND VENUS

AZTEC

Tonatiuh, sun god.
Metzli, moon god.
Tlahuizcalpantecuhtli (god of dawn, Venus as Morning Star), a form of Quetzalcóatl.
Xólotl (double of Quetzalcóatl), associated with Venus as Evening Star.

MAYA

Kinich Ahau, sun god by day. Jaguar god of the Underworld, sun god by night.
Ix Chel (Goddess Rainbow), goddess of the moon.
Lahun Chan, god of Venus.

Xipe Totec   *Xochipilli*

EARTH AND FERTILITY

AZTEC

Xipe Totec (god of vegetation and spring, transitions and oppositions) also known as Red Tezcatlipoca, linked with east.
Chicomecóatl, maize goddess.
Cihuacóatl, fertility goddess.
Cintéotl, maize god.
Coatlícue, earth goddess.
Tlatecuhtli, earth god/goddess.
Xilonen, maize goddess.
Xochipilli, the flower prince.
Xochiquetzal, flower goddess, also goddess of weaving.
Toci, earth goddess, also childbirth.
Teteoinnan, earth goddess.
Mayahuel, maguey plant goddess.
Ilamatecuhtli, ancient mother goddess.
Tepeyollotl, regeneration.
Tonantzin, mother goddess.
Tlazoltéotl, goddess of love and filth.

Kinich Ahau   *Ix Chel*

MAYA

Yum Caax, sometimes Young Maize God; in *Popol Vuh*, One Hunahpú.

DEATH AND DESTINY

AZTEC

Tezcatlipoca, god of night and destiny, also associated with kingship, creation, destruction, deception, war.

MAYA

Ah Puch, death god.
Ixtab, goddess of suicide.

Tlazolteotl   *Yum Caax*

MOUNTAINS

AZTEC

Popocatépetl.
Ixtaccíhuatl.
Mount Tláloc.
Tetzcotzingo.
Matlalcueye.

ANIMAL/BIRD DEITIES

AZTEC

Xólotl, dog-double of Quetzalcóatl.

MAYA

Hun Batz and **Hun Chouen**, Monkey-man gods, half-brothers of Hero Twins.
Vulture god.
Fox god.
Rabbit god.
Jaguar god figures worshipped from Olmec times onward.
Seven Macaw.
Zotz, bat god.

Tláloc

Chalchiúhtlicue

Chac

Yacatecuhtli

RAINS, WINDS, WATERS

AZTEC

Tláloc, rain god.
Tlaloques, rain gods.
Quetzalcóatl, storms and wind, also known as White Tezcatlipoca, linked with west, amid many other attributes.
Tepictoton, rain god.
Éhecatl, wind god, form of Quetzalcóatl.
Chalchiúhtlicue, goddess of springs, rivers and the sea.
Huixtocíhuatl, salt goddess.
Atl, god of water.

MAYA

Chac, rain god.

HUNTING

AZTEC

Camaxtli, hunt god.
Mixcóatl, ancient hunt god.

FIRE

AZTEC

Huehuetéotl, old fire god.
Xiuhtecuhtli, fire god.
Chantico, earth goddess.

WAR

Huitzilopochtli, México tribal god, also associated with sun and war. Also known as Blue Tezcatlipoca, linked with south.
Tezcatlipoca, associated with north.

TRADERS

AZTEC

Yacatecuhtli, god of traders and travellers.

MAYA

Ek Chuah, god of merchants.

ANCESTRAL GODS/CULTURE HEROES ETC

AZTEC

Quetzalcóatl-Topiltzin, god of storms, wind and rain, among many other attributes.
Huitzilopochtli, tribal god of México.
Mixcóatl, hunt god worshipped in both Huexotzingo and Tlaxcala.
Camaxtli, hunt god of Chichimec origin, worshipped particularly in Huexotzingo.

MAYA

Hero Twins Hunahpú and **Xbalanqué**.

MEDICINE AND FOODS

AZTEC

Octli, deities of pulque drink.
Patécatl, medicine god.

MAYA

Ix Chel, moon goddess, also goddess of medicine.

UNDERWORLD

AZTEC

Mictlantecuhtli, god of underworld or Mictlán.
Mictlantecacihuatl, goddess of underworld or Mictlán.

MAYA

Cizin, underworld god.
Lords of Xibalba.

Huitzilopochtli

Quetzalcóatl

Hero Twins Hunahpú and Xbalanqué

ONE ABOVE ALL OTHERS: THE SUPREME GOD?

Mesoamericans worshipped a bewildering number of gods. Each deity could simultaneously take many forms. For example, a Maya divinity might be old and young, male and female, have both spiritual and bodily forms and have animal, human and divine characteristics.

WHY SO MANY GODS?

Mesoamericans happily took on the forms of worship of previous generations. Peoples did this partly in order to legitimize their own standing. The México, for example, were keen to associate themselves with the deities and achievements of their Toltec forerunners. In addition, new gods regularly joined the pantheon. The idea of converting new worshippers to the faith, so central to Christianity, was alien to Mesoamerican thought. When the Aztecs conquered lands during the expansion of their empire, they did not suppress the gods of the native peoples. They would occasionally impose the worship of their

Below: Builders of Classic Maya cities paid frequent homage to Chac, god of rain, as here in the 'nunnery quadrangle' at Uxmal.

Right: Itzamná, the supreme Maya god, holds a vision serpent in this limestone tablet, c.100BC–AD250.

own warlike tribal god Huitzilopochtli, but they usually let their new subjects to continue their traditional forms of worship.

Many deities of the Aztecs and Maya had their origins far in the distant Mesoamerican past. The Aztec cult of the earth mother, worshipped as Tonantzin ('Our Sacred Mother') and Toci ('Our Grandmother'), might have grown from ancient rites in honour of figures of fertility goddesses, which have been found in many parts of the Mesoamerican region and dated to as far back as *c.*2000BC. In the era of the Olmec civilization (*c.*1500–400BC) Mesoamericans were already worshipping primitive forms of Tláloc (the Aztec rain god), Tezcatlipoca (the Aztec god of night and bringer of discord), Quetzalcóatl (the Aztec Plumed Serpent, known as

Kukulcán to the Maya) and Huehuetéotl (the Aztec fire god). The Olmec were devotees of a cult of the jaguar that seems to have been associated both with fertility and royalty and which had a major influence on Maya and Aztec religion. The jaguar was later a major manifestation of Tezcatlipoca.

The builders of Teotihuacán, the city so revered by the Aztecs, worshipped Quetzalcóatl, Tláloc and the rain god's consort Chalchiúhtlicue. The cult of the rain god was also strong among the Zapotec, who worshipped him as Cocijo; the Preclassic Maya knew him as Chac.

A SUPREME DIVINITY?

Certain Maya and Aztec traditions held that a supreme creator existed behind the massed ranks of the gods. According to some Maya sources, the supreme god was Itzamná ('Lizard House'), sometimes

---

TEMPLE TO THE HIDDEN GOD

Netzahualcóyotl, ruler of Texcoco, made a remarkable break with religious orthodoxy when he decided to order the construction of a temple to an abstract creator god, the source of life.

Netzahualcóyotl was the same royal figure who, as a prince, had witnessed the slaughter of his father Ixtlilxóchitl by Tepanec forces after a failed revolt and who later enthusiastically performed the ritual sacrifice of his Tepanec enemy Maxtla. He was no stranger either to bloodshed or to conventional Aztec religious life. However, he must have been touched by visions of a serene divinity, for he

built in his city-state a nine-storey temple to an abstract god he named Ipalnemoani ('The One By Which We Live') or Tloquenahuaque ('The One Who is Always Near').

The shrine to this deity, situated at the top of the temple, was empty of statues or other conventional decoration, for the Texcocan ruler believed the god he wished to celebrate could not be ascribed a visible form. Netzahualcóyotl showed a typically Mesoamerican openness to divergent religious approaches by allowing the other major Aztec gods to be worshipped on the lower levels of his temple.

known also as Hunab Ku ('Only Spirit'). He was depicted as a great sky serpent or as an old man, toothless and with a hooked nose, and was believed to be patron of writing and divination. His consort was Ix Chel ('Lady Rainbow'), goddess of childbirth, medicine and weaving.

Similarly, one Aztec creation myth told of a supreme creator, Ometéotl, who brought the Earth into being. Ometéotl had dual male-female aspects, was known as 'Lord of Duality' and could manifest as separate deities, Tonacatecuhtli ('Lord of Our Sustenance') and Tonacacíhuatl ('Lady of Our Sustenance'), who were entwined in a fruitful embrace. In different versions of the myth, either Ometéotl created the family of Aztec gods or Tonacatecuhtli made the Plumed Serpent Quetzalcóatl from his breath.

Another prominent Aztec ruler, Netzahualcóyotl, King of Texcoco, is reported to have been drawn to the worship of an abstract and supreme deity. However, both cultures were, in general, polytheistic. The concept of one god above or encompassing all others was largely foreign to the Mesoamerican imagination.

CHANGING SIGNIFICANCE
Scholars have shown the Maya worshipped different supreme deities in different eras and perhaps different groups.

Left: A Zapotec gold pendant depicts (top to bottom) the ball game; the sun; a knife representing the moon and an early form of Tlaltecuhtli, the Earth Monster of Aztec myth.

Right: Scholars often identify this basalt deity as Ometéotl, the Aztec 'Lord of Duality'.

Itzamná and the bird deity Seven Macaw were revered as the highest of gods in the early days of Maya civilization, but later on Seven Macaw alone was worshipped in this way. Yet in the *Popol Vuh* of the Quiché Maya, Seven Macaw is no more than a boastful fraud and the Quiché acclaim the one-legged fire god Tohil as the supreme divinity.

A variant Aztec creation legend tells the story of how a multiplicity of gods was born. A primeval goddess gave birth to a *técpatl* or sacrificial knife, which fell on to the northern plains that were the land of origin of the Aztecs' Chichimec ancestors. As it hit the hard ground in that inhospitable desert place, gods beyond number were born and spread out to fill the earth.

THE BLOOD OF MANY

One of the most important religious ceremonies of the year in Tenochtitlán was Panquetzalíztli, held to honour Huitzilopochtli, the divine leader of the Aztec state and unique to the México. Panquetzalíztli was held after the harvest, when the nation readied itself for war.

BATHED SLAVES

Many captive warriors of subject peoples were put to the knife before the shrine of Huitzilopochtli. Other victims were so-called 'bathed slaves', who had been purchased at market by successful merchants and offered for sacrifice in the hope of winning divine blessing. The slaves were often picked for their good looks and musical or dancing ability, for in the build-up to the festival they had to entertain guests at magnificent feasts thrown by the merchant for senior traders and noblemen. Nine days before Panquetzalíztli, the slaves were washed in a spring sacred to Huitzilopochtli and began religious preparation for their own

Below: A tzompantli *or skull rack for displaying victims' heads stood atop the Great Pyramid in Tenochtitlán.*

sacrifice. On the day of the festival, the slaves were led four times around the Great Temple then, in the company of the merchant-donor, they climbed the temple's steep steps to the shrine of Huitzilopochtli at the top. There, a priest dressed as Huitzilopochtli dispatched them. They were spreadeagled across the sacrificial stone, the chest was sliced open and the heart torn from its cavity. The merchant was awarded the bodies, and afterwards he would take them back to his house to be consumed with maize in a cannibalistic banquet.

VICTIMS BECOME GODS

Each of the Aztec months was sacred to a particular deity and, at the end of each month, victims dressed as the god in question were respectfully slaughtered. The victims, known as *ixiptla* ('in the god's image'), became the gods they honoured and were treated with the greatest reverence and ceremony. They were said to hold the fire of the god in

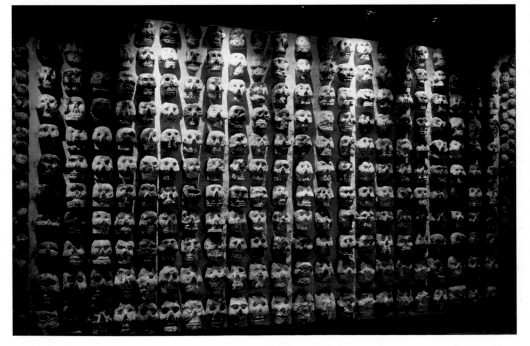

Left: The wooden handle of this sacrificial knife is covered with a mosaic of turquoise, malachite, shell and mother-of-pearl.

their bodies, and when they were slaughtered this divine flame was set free to take residence in the body of a victim marked for sacrifice in a year's time.

Perhaps the most remarkable of these ceremonies was that held to honour Tezcatlipoca. Each year, at the close of the month holy to Tezcatlipoca, a young man of intelligence and good looks was selected to represent the god and for a year was treated as his embodiment. By day, he lived in the god's temple, where he learned to play the flute and dance steps sacred to the 'Lord of the Smoking Mirror'. By night, he was sent out into the city, accompanied by a guard of eight warriors. In every quarter he visited he played evocative tunes on his flute, shaking the rattles tied to his legs and arms as he danced to signal his coming. The people of Tenochtitlán would nod reverently and sometimes carry out sick children to be blessed and cured by the passing god.

As the year drew to an end, the preparations for the sacrifice intensified. The Emperor visited Tezcatlipoca's temple and dressed the young man in the costume sacred to the god.

The god-victim was given four young wives, embodiments of significant goddesses. With five days to go to the sacrifice, the *tlatoani* or ruler went into devout retreat and the people understood that Tezcatlipoca was governing the Aztec capital of Tenochtitlán.

Above: Worshippers gaze reverently up the pyramid's steep steps as a victim's warm heart is flung skywards to honour the gods.

On the final day of the month, the youth was led with full ritual to Tezcatlipoca's shrine on the Great Pyramid. There he said goodbye to his four divine consorts, was placed over the sacrificial stone and his heart was pulled from his body. His corpse was taken down the steps and a meal of his cooked flesh served to the *tlatoani* and most prominent of the city's nobility and military elite. One of those in the select company was the young man who had been chosen to carry Tezcatlipoca's sacred flame within his body for the following 20 Aztec months – and be slaughtered in the god's name on the same day the following year.

Solar eclipses were terrifying times for the Aztecs, suggesting the unnatural encroachment of night into day, and *tzitzimime*, vengeful female spirits associated with darkness, were believed to rise in power. They could send sickness epidemics and were expected to play a part in the destruction of the Fifth Sun at the end of the current age. At times of eclipse, Aztecs made offerings of their own blood to persuade the god to sustain the sun and life on Earth. People with fair complexions were said to be full of light and were sacrificed to strengthen the sun in its struggle against darkness.

The Aztecs also held frequent sacrifices in the name of the rain gods, the *tláloques*. The gods cruelly required the blood of young children. As they were led to their deaths, the children would weep and the onlookers understood the tears that fell would become the rain they prayed for.

Right: On a pre-Toltec stela carved at the Maya site of Santa Lucia, Guatemala, a priest holds a severed head that drips blood.

COMMUNION WITH THE DIVINE

Sacrificial victims were treated with the greatest reverence. When an Aztec warrior captured a prisoner who would be taken to a ritual death, he treated him with solemnity and respect, declaring, 'Here I find my well-loved son'. A prisoner taken in this way was also said to take a grim satisfaction in the event and to declare, 'Here I encounter my well-respected father.' The only honourable fate for a warrior was to kill or be killed in battle or, if captured alive, to be taken to the temple for ritual death.

TLAHUICOLE

The story of the Tlaxcaltec warrior named Tlahuicole graphically demonstrates this concept. So great was Tlahuicole's renown in battle that, when he was captured by Aztec warriors, the *tlatoani* decided to spare his life and give him command of the Aztec army in a campaign against the Tarascans. Tlahuicole took on the command as he was ordered, but when he returned from the field he asked to be put to ritual death, for he felt that living on in captivity shamed him, whereas his sacrifice would restore the honour he had laboured so hard to win.

Below: A Yaxchilán lintel shows Lady Xoc having an ecstatic encounter with the Vision Serpent after sacrificing her own blood.

Above: Sacrificial rituals presented a magnificent spectacle, with sacred music and extravagant costumes on display.

MESSENGERS TO THE GODS

Those killed in ritual sacrifice were seen as messengers to the gods or were sometimes understood to become the very gods in whose honour they were put to death. Both priests and victims sometimes dressed as the gods they honoured and, among the Aztecs, victims were sometimes declared to be *ixiptla* ('in the god's image'). In this sense, the sacrificial ritual was a way of honouring and renewing the divine presence on Earth. The gods entered and united with the bodies of the victims and so were made manifest before the watching crowds.

The sacrifices presented a magnificent spectacle. Priests were bedecked in splendid costumes and feather headdresses and flowers adorned the temples. Musicians performed on conch-shell trumpets, flutes made from bones or reeds, drums and rattles. Dancers wore gold and silver bells that made a high ringing sound and blood flowed in a bright river from the steep temple steps to the bodies of the slain piled high at the temple front.

CANNIBALISM

Among the Aztecs it was common practice for the warriors who captured prisoners in battle to feed and care for them in captivity before the sacrifice. After the ritual, the bodies were decapitated and the heads put on display on the skull rack. The cannibalistic rite in which the victorious warriors would eat the bodies particularly shocked the Spanish conquistadors. However, if we understand that the Aztecs saw the victims as touched by or even embodying the gods, then we can see the act of cannibalism as a religious ritual, an act of communion with the divine. By eating the flesh of the victim, the warriors were able to share in the offering made to Huitzilopochtli at the summit of the temple-pyramid.

RELIGIOUS ECSTASY

Maya bloodletting was sometimes seen as a mystical act, an attempt to enter an ecstatic state in which a worshipper could communicate with ancestors or gods. Celebrated carvings in the Maya city of Yaxchilán show Lady Xoc, wife of King Shield Jaguar, in a bloodletting ritual.

In the first carving, Lady Xoc is shown drawing her own blood by pulling a thorned cord across her tongue, while her husband holds a flaming torch above her head. The second carving shows that her devotions deliver her to a visionary state. The blood she has produced has been collected on a piece of bark paper and set alight, producing a swirl of smoke in whose coils she can see the awesome Vision Serpent who commands the gateway through which the supernatural becomes visible in the natural realm.

The serpent has two jaws through which ancestors or deities can make themselves known in the world of men. From one peers the head of the war god, while from the other emerges the founder of the great Yaxchilán dynasty, Yat Balam ('Jaguar Penis'). Lady Xoc is asking for the help of Jaguar Penis and the war god in a military campaign which her husband, Jaguar Shield, is preparing. The inscription alongside the carvings dates the events shown to c. AD724–726.

Religious sacrificial ritual was not intended to bring the divine from another place into the physical world. The universe was filled with spiritual presence and the many gods, with their defined powers and roles, were everywhere. The sacrificial ritual celebrated this ever-present divine power in magnificent and devout spectacle.

Below: Masked dancers, priests and musicians congregate for a sacrificial ceremony in the Maya city of Bonampak.

REACHING FOR THE SKY

To Mesoamericans, the sky was a sacred place. The rising of Venus or of the sun and the movements of the stars played out the events of mythology and the deeds of the gods. The holiest places were those such as mountain peaks or the tops of temple pyramids that were nearest to the sky. At the climax of religious festivals, reverent processions would make the steep climb to the top of the pyramids to honour the gods high above the earth.

Many Aztec pyramids had temples at many levels, with the shrines of the most revered deities situated in the holiest of places at the top. The Great Temple at Tenochtitlán, which was inaugurated with such fervour by Emperor Ahuítzotl, had twin shrines to Huitzilopochtli (decorated with white and red symbols of war) and to Tláloc (coloured with white and blue symbols of water and rain) on its summit. There were areas sacred to other deities lower down the temple.

Above: The eastern stairs on the Pyramid of the Magician at the Maya site of Uxmal climb directly from ground to sanctuary.

Below: Cortés struck a blow to Aztec hearts when his men captured and wrecked the sacred arena on top of the Great Pyramid.

HUMILIATING AZTEC DEFEAT

At the time of the Conquest, this temple-top area, the most sacred place in the entire Aztec realm, was effectively appropriated for Spain and for Christianity by Hernán Cortés in an act of astonishing bravado and symbolic weight.

After the Spaniards had taken Moctezuma captive, when the Aztec leader was still nominally in control of his empire, Cortés demanded that a place of Christian worship be established on the highest level of the Great Temple. Moctezuma, fearful for his life and playing for time in case he could effect an escape, had no choice but to agree.

A Christian cross and an image of the Virgin Mary were placed at the summit of the temple, which could be viewed from all over Tenochtitlán and could even be seen from the shores of Lake Texcoco. Beneath these sacred icons, Cortés and the most prominent of the Spanish party held a Christian Mass, while the Aztecs looked on in dismay and rising fury.

In the wake of this event, the Aztec warriors and nobility attacked the Spaniards in the Europeans' compound. Subsequently, Cortés and his conquistadors added insult to injury by storming and destroying the upper levels of the Great Temple, throwing down and burning Tláloc's and Huitzilopochtli's shrines.

Above: The main pyramid at Cobá rises to 42m (138ft). A sacred way (sacbé) runs from its base towards Chichén Itzá.

MAN-MADE MOUNTAINS

Throughout Mesoamerica, mountains were important religious symbols and sometimes also the settings for sacred rites. The Maya believed that the souls of their dead ancestors found a dwelling place in the rocky heights of mountains.

The Maya living in lowland regions erected their own peaks in the form of the steep-sided temples that dominate the magnificent ruins of Maya cities. Some of these man-made mountains were royal mausoleums as well as temples; like the pyramids of ancient Egypt, they were built primarily to house the tombs of great kings. The Aztec peoples of the Triple Alliance built shrines and celebrated important religious fertility festivals on the hills of Huixachtlán and Tetzcotzingo and on Mount Tláloc. Like the Maya, they viewed their pyramid temples as sacred peaks.

Huixachtlán ('Place of the Thorn Trees') is an extinct volcano that stands between Lakes Xochimilco and Texcoco. It was a sacred place long before the México made their way into the Valley of Mexico in the 13th century. On a temple

Right: This clay temple was probably sacred to Quetzalcóatl-Éhecatl and may have been used as a household shrine.

platform high on Huixachtlán, the Aztecs celebrated the human sacrifice that was the central event in the New Fire rites that marked the end of one 52-year cycle and the beginning of the next.

Mount Tláloc, the highest peak on the eastern rim of the Valley of Mexico, rises well above 4,000m (13,000ft) and commands awe-inspiring views of the volcanoes Popocatépetl and Ixtaccíhuatl. It, too, was a sacred spot from ancient times. The México and their allies in the Triple Alliance maintained a temple on the mountain-top where they celebrated an annual fertility rite. The rulers of Tenochtitlán, Texcoco, Tlacopán and Xochimilco made a pilgrimage to the mountain-top at the high point of the dry season to make offerings to Tláloc the rain god and usher in the rainy season. On Tetzcotzingo, a lower peak that lies in the foothills of Mount Tláloc, were several shrines to earth and maize deities. Netzahualcóyotl, the ruler of Texcoco, rebuilt and redeveloped many of these temples and shrines.

THE GREATEST OF AZTEC TEMPLES

In 1487, Emperor Ahuítzotl inaugurated El Templo Mayor, the Great Temple in Tenochtitlán, with an immense ritual sacrifice described by the chronicler Fernando de Alva Ixtlilxóchitl as, 'butchery ... without equal in human history'.

Work on the Great Temple had begun many years earlier under Moctezuma I (1440–68). To the warrior leader Ahuítzotl fell the task of dedicating a temple worthy of the gods who had delivered such a great empire to the Aztecs.

Ahuítzotl had become emperor only the previous year, in 1486, and had spent the first year of his reign in military campaigns against rebel provinces. They must have furnished many prisoners of war. Back in Tenochtitlán, the festival in honour of the Great Temple lasted for four days.

According to some sources, as many as 80,000 victims were sacrificed during the festival. From all points of the compass, seemingly endless lines of captives were led towards the temple and up its steep sides to their deaths. In the sacred area at the top, Ahuítzotl stood waiting, attended by the rulers of his imperial allies Texcoco and Tlacopán. Ahuítzotl himself made the first sacrifice, plunging his obsidian knife into the chest of the victim on the sacrifical stone, then holding the heart up to the sacred sky before making obeisances to the new shrine of Huitzilopochtli. An army of priests was ready to take over in the emperor's wake. Bodies almost beyond counting were flung down the temple steps, staining them with the blood that the Aztecs understood to be the water of life, the offering sweetest to their gods.

SPIRIT JAGUARS: SHAMANS

The religious life of Mesoamericans went beyond the public rites of sacrifice conducted by the emperor, the warrior elite and the priests in temples. The people had a strong and enduring belief in shamans. These were people gifted with visionary and religious powers who were capable of making journeys of collective psychic discovery on behalf of the tribe, who could conjure the powers of the spirit world and influence the destiny of individuals and of the city-state itself.

JAGUAR IMAGERY

Belief in shamans in the region of Mexico and Guatemala dates back at least to the Olmec civilization of *c.*1500–400BC and probably much earlier still, into the Siberian past of Mesoamerican peoples. Shamans are still active among certain Siberian and Arctic peoples, the descendants of contemporaries of the first nomads who made the trek across the Bering landmass to North America as long as 23,000 years ago.

Jaguar imagery used by Olmec craftsmen is thought to honour the shape-shifting shamans. The jaguar's furtive behaviour and deadly capacity to hunt in the hours of darkness made it one of the key allies of the shaman in his

demanding spirit-journeys. Shamans were said to be able to transform themselves into these majestic creatures during their trances.

The jaguar later became the principal animal form of the god Tezcatlipoca, the patron deity of shamans and the god of night among many other things. According to the Franciscan friar Diego Durán, a polished obsidian statue of Tezcatlipoca stood in the temple dedicated to

Left: This obsidian mirror sacred to Tezcatlipoca, god of shamans, was probably part of the treasure Cortés sent to Europe.

Above: According to myth, the Maya god Itzamná built the great Pyramid of the Magician, Uxmal, in a single night.

the god on the Great Pyramid at Tenochtitlán. The god Tezcatlipoca's image held a gold mirror, indicating that he saw everything that happened. The builders of Teotihuacán almost certainly practised shamanism like their forebears of the Olmec civilization and their cultural descendants among the Aztecs. A carving of a jaguar or other feline emerging from a doorway decorated with starfish and zigzag markings symbolic of light was found in excavations at Teotihuacán in 2001.

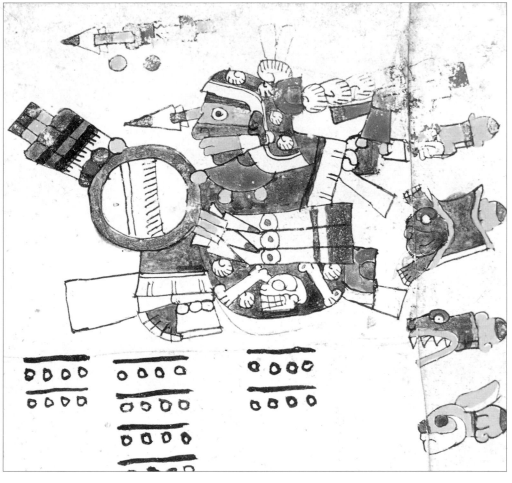

Right: An image from the Codex Cospi *(c.1350–1500) depicts the 'black aspect' of Tezcatlipoca, associated with sorcery.*

The carving is thought to represent the shaman-jaguar emerging from the spirit world on his return to the world of men after a journey. It was uncovered in the ruins that scholars believe were once a large palace, just north of the Pyramid of the Sun.

ANIMAL DOUBLES

Many Aztec gods had the capacity to appear in animal, human or other form. Tezcatlipoca, the deceiver and sower of discord, was said to appear as a coyote, a monkey or a skunk in addition to his more princely jaguar form. Moreover, Mesoamericans believed animal doubles were not the sole preserve of the gods. Each person had an animal form, a kind of animal familiar, which functioned as a protector. In the Aztecs' Nahuatl language, the animal form was called *tonal*. The word *nahual* was used to refer to the secret ability to shift shape and to the shamans who could practise it.

TRANCES AND VISIONS

From far back in Mesoamerican history, shamans took hallucinogenic substances to induce trances and visions. They made narcotic substances for ritual use from the toxin that toads make and store in small bumps on their head, as well as from the seeds of morning glory, from the peyote cactus and from various hallucinogenic mushrooms.

Some shamans were also temple priests, while others were not part of the traditional religious hierarchy. A shaman played an important role within the temple functions among the Maya. Known as a *chilam*, he was a man believed to be gifted with visionary powers. He would enter a visionary trance, after ritual bloodletting from his cheeks, earlobes or penis, and in the trance would receive and transmit messages from the gods. Other priests gathered round to translate his divinely inspired speech.

Some shamans offered to cure sickness using herbs and healing plants or native rites of magic. Others practised black magic and were deeply feared. One group of magicians known as 'sleep throwers' claimed that, through spells involving the arm of a woman who had died in child-birth, they could ensure that victims would be asleep so that a passer-by could steal from them. Other unscrupulous lay-priests promised to bring harm to enemies by burning tiny effigies of them.

THE SERPENT'S DOUBLE

Among the Aztecs, the god Xólotl's ability to change shape made him a patron of magicians and sorcerers.

In one version of the Aztec myth of the birth of the sun and moon, the assembled gods chose to sacrifice themselves in order to make these celestial bodies begin their cycle of movements across the sky. But one god, Xólotl, refused to give himself up. In his attempts to escape he transformed himself into a double ear of maize, a double maguey plant and a fish before he was caught and the gods' collective will was carried out.

Xólotl was god of monsters and of twins and other dual manifestations. He was associated with dogs, especially with the hairless dogs known as *xoloitzcuintli* by the Aztecs. Xólotl was celebrated also as the dog-double of the Plumed Serpent Quetzalcóatl and in this guise travelled with Quetzalcóatl into the underworld, Mictlán, where they succeeded in collecting the bones of past generations of humans. They later used the bones to create a human race for the new age of the world. Quetzalcóatl, of many attributes, was associated with the planet Venus and, in his form as Xólotl, was Venus rising as the evening star. Scholars believe that Xólotl was originally an independent Mesoamerican god of monsters who became associated with Quetzalcóatl in the Postclassic Period.

READING THE FUTURE

Mesoamericans believed that time was sacred, part of the substance of the gods themselves, and that those skilled in sacred rites could read the events of the future. One of the priest's key roles among both Maya and Aztecs was as a diviner of what was to come. This mystical activity had its full complement of practical applications on the level both of the city-state and of the humble farmer or merchant.

Such was the demand for information about the future that, as well as trusting in their priests, Mesoamericans also turned to a range of lay figures who offered access to arcane knowledge. Some claimed to be able to decipher patterns of future events in the shifting of light on an obsidian mirror or on water in a pot. Others could see what was to come in the lines made by a handful of maize grains when they were flung down on a cloak.

Right: A priest makes an offering. This Classic Maya stone disc (c.AD600–700) was found at Tonina in Chiapas, Mexico.

SACRED BUNDLES

Some aspects of religious life in Mesoamerica were distinctly different from the public ritual of major human sacrifices. One example is the Aztec and Maya practice of worshipping bundles that contained objects holy to a god or ancestor. This tradition may have dated back to the ancient days of migration, when nomads packed up their gods when they raised camp to move on. According to the *Popol Vuh*, the Quiché Maya brought a holy parcel with them on their migrations and worshipped it in honour of a revered ancestor, and the México and other Chichimec groups are also known to have carried sacred bundles held holy to forebears. Among the México, sacred bundles were carried by special priests named 'god-bearers'. The bundles were said to contain the mantles of the gods, which were left at the dawn of this era when the deities sacrificed themselves to give motion to the sun and moon, as well as jaguar skins, pieces of jade, jewels and other precious items. Maya of all social ranks kept life-sized clay idols for use in religious rites in the home.

RITUALS OF ATONEMENT

The need to propitiate and satisfy the gods could go beyond ritual sacrifice, whether of humans, animals or the worshippers' own blood. There were several established rituals among Mesoamericans for atonement, confession or mortification of the self. The Aztecs allowed men to make amends for sexual wrongdoing by

---

AFTER THE CONQUEST

The shapeshifting gods of Mesoamerica lived on after the conquistadors imposed Christian culture and doctrines.

The Mesoamericans were quick to take to the new faith of Christianity. They appear to have seen in the worship of Jesus Christ a similarity to the cult of the Plumed Serpent Quetzalcóatl. Jesus's teachings on brotherly love were in harmony with Topiltzin-Quetzalcóatl's pious and peaceful government, while the Christian idea of the second coming clearly resonated with the ancient Mesoamerican myth of Quetzalcóatl's departure and promised return. In an unlikely marriage of faiths, the Plumed Serpent became closely associated with Christ.

The Mesoamericans also adapted Roman Catholic Christian practices to the old faiths and continued to follow aspects of the old religion under the noses of the Christian monks. Among both Maya and Aztecs, for example, old gods were linked to Christian saints: Tláloc the rain god was revered under the guise of St John the Baptist. At the same time, traditional practices were aligned with Christian festivals: the yearly visit to the graves of the ancestors was carried out on All Souls' Day. In 1531, a peasant named Juan Diego had a vision of a dark-skinned Virgin Mary near a temple to the ancient Earth goddess Tonantzin. Under the name of the Black Virgin of Guadelupe, this hybrid Mesoamerican-Christian deity became Mexico's patron saint.

The way in which Aztecs and Maya accepted Christian practices while also maintaining the ways of the old faith is typical of Mesoamericans' approach to religion. They were generally willing to accept that new gods and new practices were an extension of what they already knew, rather than a completely new departure, and built upon existing practices and pantheons rather than replacing them.

Above: The Aztecs made regular devotions at household shrines containing clay temples and models of the gods and goddesses.

abasement before Tlazoltéotl, a fertility goddess associated with filth, excrement and sex. The individual would take his confession to a priest dressed as Tlazoltéotl and would be allowed freedom from his past deeds in return for faithful performance of penitential acts.

The Zapotecs made the rite of ritual bloodletting an occasion for confession. After making cuts in their cheeks and arms, they would let the blood flow on to husks of maize while they made a solemn statement of their evildoing.

The Maya had a scapegoat tradition, in which an individual took on the punishment for a whole community's wrongdoing. The villagers would choose one person, often an elderly woman, who would listen as each person recounted how they had shamed themselves or the group. The scapegoat would then be put to death by stoning.

Right: Fertility goddess Tlazoltéotl had the power to wipe away sexual wrongdoing. Her image is from the Codex Rios *(c.1570–95).*

DEATH AND THE AFTERLIFE

Mesoamericans had a highly developed awareness of death and its proximity. Life expectancy was low, child mortality was high, wars were frequent, if not almost continuous, and religion called for a steady stream of human victims for sacrificial rituals. Death, its rituals and speculation about a human's fate after this life inspired intriguing narratives in both Aztec and Maya mythology. Ancient Mesoamerican beliefs associated with death, sacrifice and the afterlife are as profound as those of other major civilizations. Their investigation of the human spirit's destiny after death ranks alongside the ancient Egyptian and Tibetan Books of the Dead.

Below: These solid clay figurines of elegantly attired members of the Maya nobility were left in graves on Jaina Island.

COSMOLOGY
The cosmology of both Aztec and Maya envisaged a many-layered universe, with thirteen tiers of heaven rising above the Earth and nine levels of Mictlán, a sinister underworld beneath. To the Aztecs, the underworld was a place of darkness and fear, of endless misfortune. Its rulers were the skeleton god Mictlantecuhtli, Lord of the Dead, and his serpent-skirted spouse Mictecacíhuatl.

According to the Aztecs, a select few were bound for the happy realms above. What was decisive was not how individuals lived but how they died. Those who died a natural death were bound for the underworld, but warriors killed in battle, women who died in childbirth and even those who took their own lives were spared the lower realms. Warriors who

Above: Among the Aztecs, the corpse was tied in a squatting pose prior to cremation or, for richer people, burial with grave goods.

died on the battlefield became *cuauhteca* ('Eagle Companions') and could enter the eastern paradise Tonatiuhichán. They were destined to join the entourage of the great sun himself in the form of hummingbirds or butterflies.

One tradition told that the souls of these great men were responsible for the daily miracle of the sun's return. At dawn and throughout the morning hours, the spirits of warriors slain on the battlefield hauled the sun up from its nightly residence in the underworld to its position at its zenith in the sky. Those who died by water or in storms – for example, by drowning or by lightning – were said to be destined for Tlalocán, a paradise presided over by the great rain god Tláloc, where life-giving waters fell in a constant light drizzle and flowers, fruit and delectable foods grew abundantly without need for the human labour of irrigation, digging and planting.

The Maya also believed that some would progress to a life of heavenly ease. Shaded by the strong boughs of the world's first tree, they would enjoy their leisure drinking chocolate. However, the

great majority were destined for the dark and dangerous realms of the underworld. The Maya called this dread place Xibalba ('Realm of Fright'). Here the dead would have to undergo many trials at the hands of foul and sadistic divinities.

FUNERARY RITES

Both rich and poor were buried with supplies to help them on this afterlife voyage. Poorer Maya were laid beneath the floors of their house. People were buried with the tools of the trade they followed. For example, hunters would be interred with their spears and fishermen with their harpoons and nets. The dead were also supplied with pottery containers of water and food supplies. Most would also have a little ground maize placed in their mouth and a handful of jade beads for use as money in the world after death. After an entire generation of burials, the house would no longer be used for daily living and would be kept as an ancestral shrine.

Below: A tomb in the Maya city of Uxmal marks the spot at which the deceased noble began his journey to the underworld.

Nobles, royalty and the priestly elite were buried in splendid tombs with generous supplies and even helpers. A Maya nobleman buried at Tikal was surrounded by fine ceramic vessels that contained maize stew and chocolate drink. He was accompanied by the bodies of nine servants who had been sacrificed at his death. Many took worldly wealth with them on their journey, presumably in the hope of using it during their underworld ordeals. A priest buried at Chichén Itzá was adorned with a splendid necklace of pearls that may have been brought from as far away as Venezuela by traders. The rulers and nobility were buried in the great plazas of the Maya cities. The Maya understood that the voyage to the underworld began by water, and nobles were often depicted travelling to the lands below by canoe. The great plazas were seen as symbolic lakes that gave access to the land of the dead below.

In Yucatán, some members of the nobility were cremated. Their ashes were placed in pottery or wooden urns carved with the dead person's features.

Above: To the Aztecs, death was a frequent visitor. This decorated child's skull was offered to Mictlantecuhtli, god of the dead.

Sometimes portrait statues were commissioned. These were left with a hollow space in the back of the head in which to place the ashes.

Most Aztecs were cremated. The corpse was dressed in his or her best clothes, then tied in a squatting pose and wrapped in cloth before being set alight. Interment in stone vaults was reserved for prominent members of the nobility and rulers. As among the Maya, a notable man might have a number of servants and even wives killed on his death so that they could accompany him to the underworld.

Among both Aztecs and Maya, a dead man was sometimes buried with his dog to provide a companion and protector-guide on his journey. The custom had religious and mythological resonance, for the revered deity Quetzalcóatl was accompanied by his dog-twin Xólotl on his journey to the underworld.

CHAPTER FOUR

WARFARE AND MILITARY LIFE

War was a way of life for Mesoamericans. The Aztecs waged war for practical gain to secure resources, raw materials and slave labour. They also understood that to wage war was to be intimately connected with the religious duty to return energy to the cosmos and to make devotions to the gods through offerings of lifeblood. Military might was an instrument of empire, used to conquer territory and deter rebellion, and also a means of capturing victims for the sacrificial knife. Some Aztec campaigns were conducted for this purpose above all others. It was not markedly different among the Maya. Classic-Period inscriptions and surviving texts suggest rival Maya city-states were almost constantly in conflict. Like the Aztecs, the Maya were hungry for live prisoners; ordinary folk were earmarked as slave labourers and the nobles among the captives were destined for sacrifice on the temple-pyramids.

War was therefore understood as a natural condition by both the Aztecs and the Maya. The great god Huitzilopochtli leapt from his mother Coatlícue's body fully armed and immediately began to wield his weapons, slaughtering his sister Coyolxauhqui, the moon goddess, and hundreds of his brothers in the first moments of his life. The Aztecs saw their male offspring in Huitzilopochtli's image, envisaging them as warriors from the day of their birth, or even before. Women who died in childbirth were understood to have perished at the hands of their unborn offspring.

Left: Toltec stone warriors at Tula stand 4.6m (15ft) tall. Ready for battle, each carries an atlatl *spear-thrower.*

THE FLOWER WARS

Some Aztec military campaigns were planned in advance and carried out with the agreement of both sides as a testing ground on which warriors could capture prisoners for religious sacrifice. Such a battle was known as *xochiyaóyotl* ('war of flowers') in reference to the magnificently dressed warriors rounded up and carried home like a garland of blooms.

Some scholars believe that the practice originated in the distant Mesoamerican past, but no examples have yet been found of Toltec or earlier wars conducted solely to capture live prisoners. Among the earliest known instances of *xochiyaóyotl* is the war between the México/Tepanecs and the Chalca, which began in 1376 and which is believed to have started as a 'flower war'.

BUYING FOOD AT MARKET

In the 1400s, the city-states of the Triple Alliance conducted regular campaigns of this kind against Atlixco, Huexotzingo and other cities. Tlacaélel, brother of Moctezuma I Ilhuicamina (1440–1468), likened the gathering of victims through war to buying food at market.

Discussing plans for the inauguration of the Great Temple in Tenochtitlán and the constant need for a plentiful supply of sacrificial victims, Tlacaélel declared that there was no actual need for their war god Huitzilopochtli to wait for an insult, diplomatic quarrel or some other conventional reason to start a war: he should simply find and enter a convenient 'market' for

Right: A Totonac carving from east-central Mexico shows a prisoner of war bound hand and foot.

Above: Images of soldiers at Bonampak show that fighting was at close quarters using spears.

the food he needed. At this market, Tlacaélel said, Huitzilopochtli and his army could gather victims like so many tortillas. The market should be nearby, because the flesh of distant peoples might not be to his liking.

Rather than fight in such distant realms as the lands of the Huastecs, the army should take their war to the conveniently situated cities of Atlixco, Tecoac, Cholula, Huexotzingo, Tlaxcala and Tliluhquitepec. The war against local enemies should not be decisive. Fighting must always continue or be easily renewed, so that Huitzilopochtli would have the victims for whom he hungered within easy reach. Huitzilopochtli would feed on them with pleasure, as a man enjoys a tortilla warm from the oven.

ESCAPE TO VICTORY

On the night of 30 June 1520, canoe-borne Aztec warriors swarmed around Spanish conquistadors as the Europeans attempted to flee Tenochtitlán along one of the many causeways that connected the city to the mainland. The Aztecs had the Spaniards at their mercy, but they did not finish them off. Instead, they allowed the surviving conquistadors to proceed on to Tlaxcalán and once there prepare for a renewed assault on Tenochtitlán.

In the darkness of the *Noche Triste* ('sad night') on 30 June, the Aztecs were in familiar surroundings while the invaders were panicking on the narrow causeway in driving rain. The defenders of Tenochtitlán had the chance to exterminate the Spaniards. Instead, they directed their attention to seizing booty and capturing prisoners. Their decision would lead to the collapse of their empire, the end of their Mesoamerican world.

Above: Battling for honour and to feed the gods, Aztec soldiers round up prisoners destined for sacrifice in Tenochtitlán.

A WAR GAME?

Some scholars suggest that the flower wars of the Aztecs might have had their origins in a kind of war game, a substitute for full conflict in which the contestants would put their fates in the hands of the gods. Historians have compared the practice to the ball game. This distinctive sport, which was practised throughout the Mesoamerican region, was seen, among other things, as a ritual enactment of cosmic struggles between good and evil or light and darkness; a kind of mythic encounter between Quetzalcóatl and his dark brother Tezcatlipoca and also between the Hero Twins and the lords of Xibalba.

Given the demand for sacrificial victims, the war game of the flower wars might have grown into a major military event, regularly conducted and leading to the deaths of thousands of warriors. Other experts suggest that the flower wars had a political and a religious dimension and were an important instrument of government. According to this theory, the wars maintained control over enemies by capturing and eliminating the leading warriors and nobles in the enemy group. It might be that in some flower wars, military and strategic aims existed alongside religious and ritual ones. Certainly, the demonstration of the Triple Alliance's military might can only have helped to discourage rebellion among subject peoples.

The flower wars took place alongside other more conventional types of conflict. The Triple Alliance regularly used its military might to extend the territory of the empire by winning land, enforcing alliances and also ensuring tribute payments were made. The religious and ritual elements so evident in the flower wars informed the Aztec approach to all types of conflict. Some historians have even suggested that the Mesoamerican understanding that ritual triumph was more important than all-out victory, was a major reason why the Aztecs were ultimately undone by Cortés's small force of conquistadors.

Below: Prisoners of the flower wars knew they had no chance of escape, but they were treated with respect. The illustration is from the Florentine Codex *(1575–77).*

CHAIN OF COMMAND: THE AZTEC ARMY

The *tlatoani* or ruler was the chief army commander. He was expected to demonstrate his own battlefield prowess by leading a military campaign as part of his coronation celebrations. His chief adviser on military matters was the *cihuacoatl* ('female serpent'). This was a position of supreme importance. Tlacaélel, the brother of Moctezuma I Ilhuicamina – who made such an eloquent statement of the values lying behind the flower wars – was *cihuacoatl* to five successive rulers of Tenochtitlán: Itzcóatl, Moctezuma I Ilhuicamina, Axayácatl, Tizoc and Ahuítzotl.

Next in command was a council of four noblemen: the *tlacochcalcatl*, the *tlaccatecatl*, the *tillancalqui* and the

Right: The ocelot, a native wild cat, was the symbol adopted by one group of Aztec warriors.

Below: In a violent phase of its cycle, the planet Venus shoots an ocelot-warrior. This detail is from a Mixtec document, the Codex Cospi.

etzhuanhuanco. They were usually brothers or near relatives of the *tlatoani* himself. Top-ranking warriors reported directly to the council members.

MILITARY ORDERS

The military was the prime promoter of social mobility among the Aztecs. A warrior from the common ranks could rise to all but the very highest army positions by dint of bravery and success in battle. The two supreme orders of warriors were the *cuauhchique* ('Shaved Ones') and the *otontin* ('Otomies'). To be admitted, a warrior must have carried out 20 or more deeds of remarkable bravery and, naturally, also have brought home a great number of prisoners for sacrifice. The elite groups of the jaguar-warriors and the eagle-warriors were members of these top-ranking groups. These elites made the most of their right to wear the feathers, jewellery and cloaks that were emblems of their high standing. In Tenochtitlán, the eagle- and jaguar-warriors had

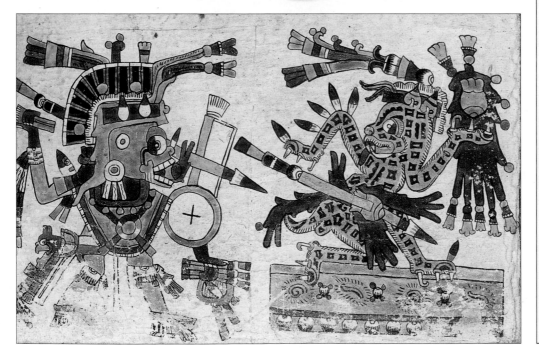

EAGLE-WARRIORS AND JAGUAR-WARRIORS

One of the many versions of the myth explaining the creation of the Sun and Moon accounts for the appearance of the eagle and jaguar in whose honour the elite warriors were named.

On the plain before Teotihuacán the twin gods Tecciztécatl and Nanahuatzin stood before the sacred fire. Would they throw themselves into the flames in order to light the world?

Tecciztécatl, haughty and boastful and dressed in magnificent robes, went forward four times to sacrifice himself, yet each time pulled back, afraid. However, his twin Nanahuatzin, humble and weak, an insignificant figure in paper clothes made from tree-bark, flung himself fearlessly into the blaze, creating the Sun. Then Tecciztécatl, inspired by the other's bravery, finally leapt into the flames, becoming the Moon.

Nanahuatzin, the twin who turned out to be the brave one despite his feeble appearance, became the patron deity of twins.

The eagle was the first creature to follow the gods Tecciztécatl and Nanahuatzin into the blaze. Forever afterwards his beautiful feathers were blackened. The jaguar followed the eagle into the fire. His burning gave his coat black spots that sometimes form a line along his back.

These brave creatures, first into the holy flames that had frightened Tecciztécatl, were worthy exemplars for the elite groups of the eagle- and jaguar-warriors of the Aztec army. If warriors proved that they knew no fear, then they were permitted to adorn themselves to accentuate their likeness to their animal forebears.

meeting houses within the temple precincts. Here, young boys were initiated into the military way of life from an early age. While still at school, the boys were taught how to handle their weapons, march on campaign and manoeuvre in battle. They learned the importance of discipline and obedience to the military hierarchy and practised using the clubs, shields, darts and spears that were used on the battlefield. The impressively dressed elite warriors mingled with them, sharing tales of their exploits on campaign and cementing the boys' love of army life. Later the boys would compete for the chance to carry equipment and other loads into battle for the elite warriors.

DUTY TO THE EMPIRE

The Aztecs had no standing army; the military hierarchy called up warriors for campaigns as necessary. Each *capultin* – a town or area of a city, based on old tribal clans – was required to provide a unit of around 400 men. They were commanded by a local leader and marched under their

Right: An Aztec terracotta statue shows an eagle-warrior ready for combat. Eagle-warriors were dedicated to 'feeding' the sun with the blood of prisoners.

own standard, but were also grouped in larger divisions of around 8,000 warriors. As many as 25 divisions would be sent on longer campaigns, making a total of 200,000 fighting men.

Before a campaign began, the supreme council dispatched orders for supplies to be collected. Tribute-paying areas had to provide beans, salt, pumpkin seeds, maize meal and maize cakes to feed the army. Army porters carried these supplies.

ON CAMPAIGN

The army would march in a long, ordered procession along the narrow roads of the Aztec empire on its campaigns. Leading the way were the army's barelegged scouts, identifiable by their simple loincloths and shirts of white cotton, faces painted with yellow ochre and long hair tied with red ribbons. They were armed with spears and carried conch-shell trumpets, which they used when they needed to send messages to the main ranks of the army behind. With them marched the warrior-priests carrying images of Huitzilopochtli, the martial god in whose name the empire's wars were waged. They were followed by the top warriors and members of the military elite. This group would include the *tlatoani* himself, if he were leading the campaign, together with members of the supreme council.

The army units from Tenochtitlán came next in the train, followed by troops from Tlatelolco, Texcoco and Tlacopán and any other currently allied cities. In the rearguard, many miles down the road from the beginning of the procession, came the troops provided by subject cities of the empire as part of their tribute payment. So narrow were the tracks the army followed that an army unit of 8,000 men might stretch out for as much as 25km (15 miles), according to leading historians.

Left: An illustration from the Codex Mendoza *(c.1541) represents six triumphs in the career of a successful warrior.*

INTO BATTLE

Ordinary members of the Aztec army wore a simple wrapping around their thighs and loins and were given a mantle or overgarment of maguey cloth. Some went barefoot into battle adorned with body paint.

HOW THEY FOUGHT

Aztec warriors fought hand-to-hand with stabbing javelins and clubs fitted with blades of the volcanic glass obsidian, protecting themselves with leather-fringed shields. Some of the older or elite warriors wore wooden helmets carved with the symbols of the order to which they belonged. They also used the *atlatl* or spear-thrower, a spear carved with a holding place for a dart. With practice, a warrior could send these darts over great distances with deadly accuracy. The *atlatl* was usually a functional object, made from plain wood for use in battle. But it also had ceremonial uses, and archaeologists have found splendid carved and painted, even gold-covered, spear-throwers. These were probably used by priests impersonating the gods during religious ceremonies.

In a typical battle, the two armies lined up opposite one another on the battlefield. There would have been a blaze of colour as the light caught on plumes and the spears waved by warriors dressed in bright animal skins. The men demonstrated their

Above: These two magnificent examples of the Aztec warrior's atlatl, *or spear-thrower, are covered with gold and carved with scenes depicting ritual sacrifices.*

fearlessness by urging the enemy to do their worst or by dashing out from their own ranks to adopt a threatening or insulting pose. Excitement built as the men's voices rose to a steady roar. The blowing of the conch-shell trumpets

---

GLADIATORIAL SACRIFICE

A sacrificial ritual celebrating the power of the Aztec warrior was the climax of the festival of Tlacaxipehualiztli ('Flaying of men')held in honour of Xipe Totec, 'Our Lord, the Flayed One', god of spring and vegetation.

In the rite, which the Spanish called 'gladiatorial sacrifice', five prisoners of war were put to death by elite Aztec warriors in a staged conflict. The prisoners, treated as always among the Aztecs with the greatest respect and even reverence as divine offerings, were dressed in a costume that identified them as Xipe Totec and tied to a sacrificial stone. They were given a club covered with feathers with which to defend themselves. Five warriors – two eagle-warriors, two jaguar-warriors and a fifth of either order who was left-handed – were set loose upon them. The battle must have been short, for the warriors fought fiercely with *macáhuitl* (clubs with obsidian blades). The blood of the sacrificed prisoners fed the earth. The Tlacaxipehualiztli festival took place in the build-up to the rainy season. Also as part of Tlacaxipehualiztli, a group of prisoners were slain by the usual method of having their heart ripped from their chest. The bodies were then stripped of their skin. Priests wore the flayed skin in honour of Xipe Totec for 20 days.

Right: A detail from the delicate carving on an Aztec huehuetl, *or wooden drum, represents a jaguar-warrior in his finery.*

Right: Unlike Cortés and his men, the Aztecs did not have iron armour. A ceramic model gives a detailed impression of the protective jerkins worn by Aztec warriors.

spilled forth and the warriors burst forward, screeching and whooping with bloodlust. They hurled stones into the enemy ranks and let loose the darts from their spear-throwers, roaring as opposing warriors fell, clutching their heads or sides. When the two advancing forces met in hand-to-hand combat, warriors fought desperately with obsidian-bladed clubs which inflicted terrible slicing wounds.

REWARDS FOR VALOUR

An Aztec warrior could express his devotion to the gods through valour in battle, but there were also many worldly incentives to urge soldiers to high achievements. Those who impressed in war and won significant numbers of sacrificial captives were presented with suits of animal skin. These soldiers could win the right to drink the favourite Aztec

alcoholic drink, *pulque*, in public places, to dine in the royal palaces and to keep concubines for their pleasure. Warriors who particularly distinguished themselves, by repeatedly proving their bravery or by taking captive many scores of prisoners, might be admitted to one of the elite companies of warriors such as the jaguar- or eagle-warriors. They had the right to wear sumptuous feather headdresses, leather bracelets, jewellery and cloaks adorned with feathers and were given their marks of rank at special presentation ceremonies, often in the presence of the *tlatoani* himself. The jaguar-warriors had the right to wear a jaguar skin over their cotton body armour, while eagle-warriors wore an eagle-head helmet.

Left: A detail from the Florentine Codex *(1575–7) shows a prisoner of war making a show of defiance when surrounded by four jaguar-warriors in a gladiatorial sacrifice.*

RUNNING THE AZTEC EMPIRE

The capture of the city of Azcapotzalco and the ritual slaughter of its ruler, Maxtla, in 1428, marked the end of the Tepanec empire and the establishment of the Triple Alliance of Tenochtitlán, Texcoco and Tlacopán that was the driving force behind Aztec expansion.

Below: This stone standard-bearer was found at the heart of the Aztec empire, the Great Pyramid in Tenochtitlán. He carried a banner outside a temple honouring Huitzilopochtli, Tláloc or another major Aztec deity.

These three independent city-states shared both in the military activity needed to conquer and control the lands of the Aztec empire and in the inflow of tribute that was its reward.

CONSOLIDATION

Following the defeat of Azcapotzalco, Itzcóatl, who was the *tlatoani* or ruler of Tenochtitlán, wasted no time in attempting to consolidate the position of his city-state and of the alliance. With the assistance of forces from Texcoco and Tlacopán, Itzcóatl led a campaign to conquer the agricultural settlements of Cuitlahuac, Culhuacán, Mixquic and Xochimilco on Lake Xochimilco to the south of Tenochtitlán.

Netzahualcóyotl, the exiled prince of Texcoco who had led the capture of Azcapotzalco, had then to attend to unfinished local business, for he was not yet established as ruler of his city-state. His father, Ixtlilxóchitl, had been ruler of that city, but in 1418 had been killed in the course of a failed war against the Tepanec warrior leader Tezozómoc. For some years Netzahualcóyotl, who had witnessed his father's death, lived in hiding, but in time he won the support of his uncle, the México leader Itzcóatl, and played a major part in the war against Azcapotzalco. Now, with Itzcóatl's backing, he eliminated elements hostile to his position and re-established his family's rule in Texcoco.

EXPANSION

The armies of the Triple Alliance looked further afield and prepared for a major campaign to conquer the fertile Tlalhuica territories that lay beyond the Ajusco Mountains, well to the south of Lake Xochimilco. They raised a vast army that marched behind a company of scouts and priests across the forest-covered Ajusco range and down to the plain beyond. The tramping soldiers carried their weapons and battle-costumes, while companies of porters transported food and other supplies. They took their objective, Cuauhnahuac, the main town of the region, and returned in triumph, carrying booty and leading prisoners for sacrifice. The Tlalhuica lands had been a valuable possession of the Tepanecs, the previous imperial power. In taking them, the Triple Alliance widened its horizons, seeking to establish itself on an equal footing with the great Tepanec state established by Tezozómoc.

The Aztec empire was a network of dependencies paying tribute to the cities of the Triple Alliance but otherwise retaining a sense of their own independence. As they acquired new territories, it was the Aztecs' policy to leave the conquered rulers in place, as long as the arranged tribute was provided on time. The initial plan, formed in the reign of Itzcóatl, was to replace local rulers with centrally appointed ones. However, Netzahualcóyotl, who had first-hand experience of the intrigues and plotting of royal factions in Texcoco, argued that leaving rulers nominally in control of their domains would reduce ill-feeling and the likelihood of revolt. Itzcóatl saw the success of Netzahualcóyotl's policy in the lands controlled by Texcoco and adopted the practice himself.

SUCCESSION

Itzcóatl's successor, Moctezuma I Ilhuicamina, consolidated the gains that had been made before embarking, in 1458, on a series of military campaigns that greatly expanded the imperial possessions. He was succeeded by his grandson Axayácatl who, in a reign of 13 years (1469–81), further expanded the empire, conquering 37 towns

Above: A battle scene from the Codex Tlaxcala *shows conquistadors overcoming Aztec resistance in the region of Culhuacán.*

in the Toluca Valley, the Gulf Coast, the Puebla Valley, Guerrero and to the north of the Valley of Mexico. He was a skilled leader and soldier, who succeeded in putting down a rebellion by Tenochtitlán's neighbouring sister-city, Tlatelolco, in 1473.

SETBACKS

Axayácatl's reign was marred six years later by a major defeat, when the Tarascans of Michoacán humbled the imperial army. In two disastrous engagements near Taximaloyán (modern Charo), the 32,000-strong Aztec army was crushed. Only 200 Méxica warriors limped home to Tenochtitlán, accompanied by fewer than 2,000 comrades from Texcoco, Xochimilco and other imperial cities. Axayácatl put this defeat behind him and led a successful campaign to put down rebellions on the Gulf Coast.

Axayácatl's brother, Tizoc, became ruler of Tenochtitlán in 1481, but his reign was a military disaster. A *tlatoani* had to lead a war as part of his coronation rites: the campaign was expected to be a triumphant procession, culminating in a magnificent sacrifice of legions of newly captured victims. In Tizoc's case, the coronation war was a near-defeat that produced only 40 prisoners. He failed to build on Axayácatl's expansionist triumphs, merely putting down revolts in already conquered parts of the empire. Rebellions became more frequent as his weakness became obvious and his reign was brought to a premature end, probably by poisoning, in 1486. Despite its military failure, Tizoc's reign produced a magnificent celebration in stone of the empire and its divine mandate.

Tizoc was succeeded by his brother Ahuítzotl. A natural leader and fearless warrior, he restored the pride of the imperial army. He led a renewed expansion, capturing 45 towns and adding great sweeps of territory to the empire, notably

Oaxaca, rich in gold, painted cotton and cochineal. Under his rule, the empire stretched from the land of the Huastecs in the north to Xoconochco in the south-east and Itzapán in the south-west.

In 1502, Ahuítzotl was succeeded by Moctezuma II Xocoyotzin, the last independent ruler of the Aztec empire. Moctezuma II further expanded the empire and consolidated it by conquering territories and countries within the imperial boundaries that had not been subjugated by his predecessors. He fought wars against Tlaxcala and Huexotzingo without marked success but with the unfortunate effect of generating a profound hatred for the Aztecs in those cities. When Hernán Cortés arrived there he found willing and unexpected allies for a war against Tenochtitlán. Overall, however, his campaigns were successful. At the time of Cortés' arrival in 1519, the empire's influence covered almost 200,000sq km (77,000sq miles) and was still growing. Moctezuma believed himself to be 'master of the world'.

Below: Aztec military might was the key to enforcing the obedience and cooperation of fellow Mesoamericans within the empire.

TRIBUTE AND TRADE

Each of the three city-states of the Triple Alliance had its own tributary areas within the empire. When they fought together on joint campaigns, tribute was divided along agreed lines: 40 per cent each for Tenochtitlán and Texcoco and 20 per cent for Tlacopán. Usually, the entire tribute would be despatched to Tenochtitlán and then sorted for redistribution. On occasion, one city agreed to assign tribute from within its tributary area to another of the allies: for example, Texcoco arranged for tribute from Tepetlaoztoc, within the Texcocan region of dependency, to be paid to Tenochtitlán as a reward for military support during the Texcocan leader Netzahualcóyotl's rise to power.

Tribute was paid to individuals as well as to cities: a ruler would often reward his committed followers with the promise of tribute payments. The wealth of many prominent lords was boosted by deliveries of rare goods from distant territories.

TRIBUTE PAYMENTS

Once a city or chiefdom had accepted defeat in battle, its rulers were required to agree payment of set amounts of tribute to a fixed schedule. The Aztec conquerors would usually appoint a tribute collector to see that regular payment was made. The use or threat of violence kept tribute flowing for, if payment of tribute stopped, the armies of the Triple Alliance were mobilized to enforce the tribute agreement.

Tribute payments ranged from basic produce such as maize, beans, chillies and cotton clothing to rarer and more valuable items such as jaguar skins, gold or jade ornaments, cacao beans and brightly coloured feathers. Pages from the *Codex Mendoza* detail the tribute required of particular provinces and the schedule for its delivery. For example, Cuauhnahuac was required to send

Left: Scholars believe that this stone warrior once stood in a building celebrating the Aztecs' divinely ordained power.

Above: In an image from the Florentine Codex, *Moctezuma II watches serenely as tribute offerings are arrayed before him.*

tribute of skirts, loincloths and cloaks every six months and war costumes and decorated shields once each year.

WEALTH OF THE EMPIRE

Diego Durán's 1581 work, *History of the Indies of New Spain*, lists the great variety of tribute paid to the lords of Tenochtitlán. This included feathers and decorated blankets, mats and seats, painted cotton clothes, and also parrots, eagles and geese.

Some tributary areas sent live lions and tigers in cages, while others sent deer, quails and rabbits. Some tributary areas sent insects, including spiders, scorpions and bees in their hives. From the coastal dependencies there came seashells, coloured stones, pearls and turtleshells, and from the city workshops came metalwork in the shape of cups and bowls and plates.

Left: Tribute exacted by the Aztec imperial power from villages within the empire included corn and trees.

routes, were engaged in alliances cemented by marriage or other ties of kinship. While their rulers remained nominally in power, some of their prominent relatives and allies were required to live at court in Tenochtitlán or Texcoco and pay homage to the *tlatoani* during state celebrations. Any goods they sent to Tenochtitlán or the other cities of the Triple Alliance were treated as gifts. Itzcóatl, Netzahualcóyotl and Moctezuma I built a series of alliances through negotiation and marriage.

Below: In Tenochtitlán towering architecture and imposing statues impressed on imperial subjects the invincibility and power of the Aztecs.

The wives and courtesans of prominent Tenochtitláns benefited from tribute payments of women's blouses and elegant skirts decorated in coloured thread with designs of roses, eagles and feathers, while other tributes included the white cotton shifts worn by women who served in the temples and the plain clothing worn by servants. Forested areas, Durán wrote, were required to send in wood, charcoal and the bark of trees for use as fuel. Food tribute included maize, beans and chillies, potatoes, avocados, bananas, pineapples, plums and honey. Rose flowers and bushes were provided for the gardens of Tenochtitlán nobles. Some provinces paid tribute in war materials: padded cotton armour, wooden shields, bows and arrows, flint arrowheads, darts, slings and stones. Some areas sent building materials such as stone and lime, while the poorer provinces, which were not able to provide worthy tribute, sent women, girls and boys to be shared among the nobility as concubines and slaves.

THE FLOW OF TRIBUTE

Demand for tribute was meticulously planned to meet needs in the cities of the Triple Alliance. In the latter years of the empire, the amount of elite produce, such as jaguar skins or golden ornaments used in warrior or priestly costumes, rose as a proportion of total tribute, reflecting an increased number of far-flung provinces able to provide such goods and a growth in the nobility's taste for extravagant display.

The flow of tribute was essential to the great religious sacrifices held in cities of the Triple Alliance. Feathers and materials were used in costumes, and tributary provinces provided the building materials and labourers used to construct the temples of Tenochtitlán.

The movement of high-quality tribute goods took place alongside commercial trading by merchants. Some combined trade with information-gathering in the marketplaces of potentially rebellious cities, working as undercover spies. Merchants working on behalf of the emperor, seeking or selling elite goods, could gather important information or make significant friendships that might facilitate political alliances within the empire.

Some provinces were not required to pay tribute to a set schedule. Instead, these cities or chiefdoms, usually situated in strategic areas such as border regions or at important sites on trade

CAMPAIGNS OF MOCTEZUMA I

Moctezuma I Ilhuicamina is celebrated as the 'father of empire' who greatly expanded the Aztec lands. However, he did not begin significant campaigns of distant conquest until 18 years after his coronation in 1440. He spent those first years building and strengthening alliances within regions already conquered by Tenochtitlán and fighting a long, intermittent war against Chalco at the eastern end of Lake Chalco that ended in victory in the mid-1450s. He also faced a series of devastating famines in the years 1450–54. These ended, presumably thanks to the gods' blessing, following the New Fire Ceremony over which the emperor presided at the close of the 52-year cycle in 1454 and the rebuilding work he began on the Great Pyramid in Tenochtitlán.

THE TIZOC ABD SUN STONES

The carving known as the Stone of Tizoc, found in Tenochtitlán's ruins in 1790, projects the empire of the Triple Alliance as an enduring achievement heroically inspired by the *tlatoani* and supported by the gods of Sun and Earth.

The cylindrical stone is carved on its upper face with a sun-disc that sends rays to east, west, north and south and, at the rim, a string of all-seeing stars. On the cylinder's bottom rim four faces of the earth-goddess Tlaltecuhtli represent the land on which the Aztec army marches, balancing the upper sun image associated with Huitzilopochtli, in whose honour the armies conquer the enemy. Around the side of the stone, Aztec soldiers are represented holding prisoners from captured cities by the hair, proudly surveyed by the *tlatoani*, Tizoc, who is dressed in the regalia of the gods Huitzilopochtli and Tezcatlipoca.

Another great carved cylinder bearing an image of the sun god – known to scholars as the Sun Stone – was carved in the era of Moctezuma I and subsequently found close to the ruins of the Great Pyramid.

EARLY CAMPAIGNS

The ruler's first major campaign was into the Huastec region in the Gulf of Mexico, an area rich in natural resources. The army coped impressively with the logistical difficulties of the long march needed to take war to the northern coast and used canny tactics in pretending to retreat in order to lure local forces into a trap. After a triumphant return to Tenochtitlán, the next move was to the south-east to capture the trading centre of Coixtlahuaca in the forbidding mountain valleys of the Mixtec lands. The pretext for war was that Aztec merchants had reported being both insulted and attacked in Coixtlahuaca,

Right: This exquisite Mixtec pectoral ornament, made of gold and turquoise, represents a warrior's shield and arrows.

although the main attraction was the tribute that might be exacted from an area celebrated for its manuscript work, weaving, gold- and metalwork, and ceramics. Following careful preparations, an army of some 200,000 troops left the city of Tenochtitlán and headed south, accompanied by 100,000 porters bearing supplies. In the rugged land around Coixtlahuaca, this great force came face to face with the Mixtecs and their Huexotzingan and Tlaxcalán allies. Hostilities began with taunts, then spear-throwers and slings were brought to bear before the two armies charged. The Aztecs broke the Mixtec line, and pursued them mercilessly through the streets of Coixtlahuaca. Eventually they reached the temple pyramid, which they climbed and torched to signal their triumph. Any Mixtec warriors who escaped fled in despair to the hills, while their brothers were rounded up.

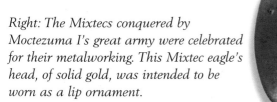

Right: The Mixtecs conquered by Moctezuma I's great army were celebrated for their metalworking. This Mixtec eagle's head, of solid gold, was intended to be worn as a lip ornament.

As the dust settled, a group of Mixtec chieftains agreed to pay tribute as a dependency of Tenochtitlán. Their ruler, Atonal, was strangled and his relatives were taken into slavery but, in the usual Aztec procedure, the other local chiefs were permitted to remain in power so long as tribute was forthcoming on the agreed schedule. The rewards for the Aztec victory included tribute of blankets, greenstone beads, feathers, gold dust, red dye, cotton, chillies and salt.

The conquerors also took home whatever they could plunder from the town, a long line of prisoners for sacrifice and religious statues from the sacked Mixtec temple. The worshippers of Huitzilopochtli would keep enemy idols 'captive' within the ceremonial area in the city of Tenochtitlán as one more sign of Aztec supremacy. Moctezuma's army returned in triumph to its homeland, its soldiers hailed as heroes by cheering crowds. The long lines of prisoners were led up the steep sides of the Great Pyramid to be dispatched in Huitzilopochtli's honour on the sacrificial stone.

Below: A detail from the Stone of Tizoc, carved during the rule of Tizoc (1469–81), shows Aztec victories over the Mixtecs.

EXTENDING THE EMPIRE

These were the first of many famous victories for Moctezuma I Ilhuicamina. The following year he sent the army eastwards to the town of Cosamaloapán, and afterwards to Ahuilzapán and Cuetlachtlán. Each time they returned in triumph, bearing tribute and plunder, having extended the might and influence of the empire and secured strategic settlements on trading routes.

When Moctezuma I Ilhuicamina's fruitful reign came to an end with the ruler's death in 1469, the Aztec lands stretched north-east to Xilotepec, east to Cosamaloapán and south to Oaxaca.

CITY-STATES IN CONSTANT CONFLICT

There was no Maya empire. Throughout the Classic Period (*c.*250BC–AD900), the city-states of the Maya lands were almost constantly at war, but no one central state emerged to establish rule over the others. Scholars liken the Maya cities to the city-states of ancient Greece: all shared a common language, religion and group of cultural assumptions, but all were strongly independent and often at each other's throats. To judge from surviving inscriptions, the dynastic ruler of a Maya state gained great prestige if he could capture a rival king, hold him captive, inflict punishing tortures on him and finally decapitate him. In the Classic Period at least, he appears not to have set much store by capturing land for himself or his subjects. The boundaries between the city-states remained largely unchanged over many years that were marked by great bloodshed.

It might be that some city-states were more powerful than others. In recent years, some scholars have suggested that

Below: Facial paint and helmet feathers impress this Maya warrior's importance and aggressive intent on his enemies.

Above: An image from a Maya codex depicts the disruption and misery of war. Two prisoners are marched into captivity.

the more powerful cities held the weaker ones in a client relationship that can be likened to the relationship between tribute-paying cities and the Triple Alliance in the Aztec empire. One of these powerful Maya cities was Calakmul. In the mid-6th century AD and afterwards it had control over Naranjo, Dos Pilas, El Perú and Cancuén. Calakmul had a great rival in Tikal and the two cities endured a long and bitter conflict.

There is also evidence that Maya cities built alliances by forging links through dynastic marriage in the same way as the Aztecs. The daughters of the nobility at Tikal, for example, appear to have made marriages with members of the ruling dynasty at Copán, Yaxchilán and Naranjo. The children of such marriages would have had strong links through their maternal family to Tikal. Scholars have demonstrated from surviving inscriptions that a noble bride from Tikal who married into the dynasty of Naranjo had a son known as Scroll Squirrel, who in turn made his wedding with a bride from Tikal, further strengthening the alliance.

HOW AND WHY THEY FOUGHT

The high-ranking Maya warrior went into battle gloriously attired. He wore a wooden helmet with brightly coloured quetzal or parrot feathers that fell across his shoulders, and painted his face with war paint. Jade jewellery around his neck and on his wrists added to the dazzling image. Maya soldiers, like the Aztecs, wore quilted jackets of cotton body armour that had been soaked in salt water to make it tougher. The Spaniards were so impressed with the effectiveness of this body protector that they adopted it in place of their own steel armour.

The principal Maya tactic was to take the enemy by surprise. The Spaniards found that Maya tactics of ambush and raiding made them a troublesome enemy. Campaigns often began with a stealthy raid into the enemy lands to seize captives. Once battle was joined, fighting was fierce, accompanied by a musical cacophony produced by the beating of drums and the blowing of whistles and conch shells. The war leaders and priests carrying divine images would occupy the centre of the battle line and were flanked by groups of foot soldiers.

Like the Aztec soldier, the Maya warrior fought mainly with a war club fitted with obsidian blades and a spear-thrower that could send darts flying over great distances when handled with skill. He also used a sling and large stones. Some accounts report that the Maya attacked by throwing fire or the nests of hornets and other stinging insects into the enemy ranks. For close-quarters fighting, the Maya warrior also had distinctive weapons in the shape of a three-pronged knife made from shell and another knife with a broad flint blade.

As among the Aztecs, warriors fought less to inflict violence than to seize booty and capture prisoners. The top prize was the ruler of a rival city. If he were

Below: A lintel at Yaxchilán shows King Shield Jaguar receiving his war gear from his wife Lady Xoc prior to battle in AD724.

captured and his capture was made known, the battle was at an end. His warriors fled if they could escape. The king faced torture and sacrificial death.

WHEN THEY FOUGHT

The fighting season was kept separate from the times of planting and harvest. Campaigns often took place in October. If they went on too long, they might well fail. There are reports of Maya campaigns fading away as the farmers fled the army to attend to their fields.

Although war was effectively continuous in that there were no prolonged periods of peace, campaigns did not need to be of particularly long duration. The Maya

Above: A Classic Maya vase (AD600–900) shows a well-equipped warrior preparing to use his spear-thrower.

city-states were small and in stark contrast to the great distances covered by the army of the Triple Alliance, a Maya force often needed to march for no more than one day to reach its enemy.

The city-states of the Maya lowlands in the Classic Period were each ruled by a dynasty that claimed descent from a historical founder and – usually – also from the gods. Each dynasty was identified by its own emblem, which would be written in inscriptions after the personal name of the ruler and his consorts.

WAR BETWEEN MAYAPÁN AND CHICHÉN ITZÁ

According to Spanish and native accounts, in the 13th and 14th centuries Mayapán was the capital of a league of city-states in northern Yucatán that also included Chichén Itzá and Uxmal. The dominant city, Mayapán, was destroyed in the 20-year period 1441–61 at the close of a struggle between tribal dynasties that had begun 250 years earlier. The dating is that given in the *Books of Chilam Balam*, which identifies events according to the Maya Short Count. (This is a variant of the Maya Long Count. The Short Count places events in 20-year periods within a cycle of 256-¼ years.) The two dynasties that came head to head were members of the Itzá people.

Below: This unsettling face was created for an incense vase found at the Itzá city of Mayapán, home to the Cocom dynasty.

WHO WERE THE ITZÁ?

In the Maya chronicles, these incomers to Yucatán are described in contemptuous terms as 'lewd ones', 'tricksters' and 'those without mothers and fathers'. They clearly did not speak the local language, because the chroniclers also called them 'people who use our tongue brokenly'. Scholars believe that the Itzá were a group of Maya who came north from the Tabasco region between Yucatán and central Mexico. The chronicles describe how they lived in the city of Chakanputún (perhaps Champotón in the coastal area of Campeche), but were driven from that place by force *c.*AD1200 and made their way north into Yucatán. They settled the city of Chichén Itzá in the period 1224–44. The Itzá renamed the city, originally called *Uucil-abnal* ('Seven Bushes'). Its new name meant 'Openings

Above: A stucco mural at Mayapán includes space for the insertion of the skull of a slaughtered prisoner of war.

of the Wells of Itzá'. They promoted the worship of the sacred well or *cenote* in the city, where offerings have been found by archaeologists. The Itzá also appear to have been devout worshippers of Ix Chel, consort of the supreme Maya deity Itzamná, in her guise as goddess of medicine.

The coming of the Itzá might have been the second settlement by Mexican incomers. Traditional histories suggest that Chichén Itzá was taken over by Toltec emigrants from Tula in AD967–987, perhaps even led by the historical prince Topiltzin who was associated with the god Quetzalcóatl. There is strong evidence of Toltec style at Chichén Itzá dating from this period. However, many archaeologists doubt whether this points to a Toltec invasion and argue that it simply represents the strength of Toltec religious and archaeological influence spread by trading contacts.

Above: The Group of the Thousand Columns was erected to surround the Temple of the Warriors at Chichén Itzá.

STRUGGLE FOR POWER

The Itzá founded Mayapán in 1263–83, leaving some of the tribe in charge at Chichén Itzá. In about 1283 the vicious quarrel between Itzá dynasties that would result in the city's downfall began. (An added complication of the dating given in the *Books of Chilam Balam* is that events are identified by their place within a 256¼-year cycle, but there is no information as to which 256¼-year period is meant. As a result, there is disagreement among scholars as to when the Itzá refounded Chichén Itzá. Some authorities believe that they settled Chichén Itzá and founded Mayapán within an earlier time cycle almost 300 years before, in AD967–87.)

The Cocom dynasty of the Itzá in Mayapán seized power from the Tutul Xiu dynasty in Chichén Itzá. The leader of the Cocom dynasty hired a mercenary army from Tabasco to enforce his will.

These soldiers, who were perhaps Toltec emigrants, swept all before them with their superior weapons. They came armed with bows and arrows, perhaps bringing them for the first time into Yucatán. Their skill with the *atlatl* or spear-thrower was extraordinary and they fought fiercely at close quarters with the spear.

The capture of the city of Chichén Itzá by this Mexican force was depicted on frescoes in Chichén Itzá and in carvings on gold discs thrown as offerings into the *cenote*. There is a marked contrast between Mexican and Maya weapons and appearance in these images. The Cocom rebuilt

Right: A clay warrior left as a grave offering on Jaina Island wears quilted cotton armour.

Chichén Itzá. The Tutul Xiu princes were driven from their city, but they did not give up. They settled near the ruins of Uxmal and nursed their hatred in exile from generation to generation, awaiting their chance. The Cocoms finally met their end in the era 1441–61.

Conspiracy made Tutul Xiu revenge possible. A Tutal Xiu chief by the name of Ah Xupán plotted with nobles in Mayapán to rise up against the Cocom chiefs. All of the Cocom princes and nobles were slaughtered. The dynasty was no more and the city of Mayapán was destroyed and left to decay.

Some Itzá exiles, however, made an enduring new home. They founded the city of Tayasal on an island in the Lake Petén Itzá in northern Guatemala. Here they survived until 1697, when they were finally conquered by the invading Spaniards.

THE MAYA COLLAPSE

In the 9th century AD, the cities of the Southern Maya Lowlands began to be abandoned. The jungle vegetation that the Maya farmers had tamed grew back and, in time, even swamped the great temples and plazas where priests and kings had celebrated royal power. Further to the north, in the Puuc Hills and towards the tip of the Yucatán peninsula, cities such as Mayapán, Uxmal, Labná and Chichén Itzá were thriving, making the decline of the lowland settlements all the more puzzling.

A HUGE HUMAN TRAGEDY

This was undoubtedly a human tragedy on a vast scale. Within four or five generations, a great civilization faded. Archaeologists and historians dubbed this remarkable development 'the Maya collapse' and for years speculated as to its causes. Why would a determined people abandon these great constructions of stone, which had been laboriously erected over many years in honour of their ancestors and gods?

THE END OF THE CLASSIC MAYA

In the years before they were left to the jungle, the Southern Lowland Maya cities one by one ended their established practice of erecting stone columns carved with the dates in the Maya Long Count of their ruling dynasties and their kings' battle victories and religious sacrifices. In archaeological terms, the Classic Period of ancient Maya civilization (c.AD250–900) is demarcated as the years during which the cities carved these stelae. The final Classic Period Maya inscription was cut in AD909.

In the cities of Yucatán in the north, meanwhile, craftsmen continued to carve inscriptions, but they did not celebrate dynastic achivements.

Above: This detail from a mural at Bonampak depicts the Maya warrior's jaguar-skin costume and feathered helmet.

Left: One of many figures of Maya warriors left in graves at Jaina Island appears serene before battle.

DIFFERING THEORIES

Archaeological evidence shows that the Maya population in the Southern Lowlands collapsed in the 9th century AD. Between AD830 and AD930, numbers fell by one third. Some writers suggested the Maya were undone by an epidemic of disease, a natural disaster such as an earthquake or hurricane, or even by an invasion.

One simplified theory is that the Maya people effectively wiped one another out in the lowlands. Centuries of almost incessant fighting between the city-states led to severe damage to the environment and greatly depleted the population. In time, the combination of falling numbers and inadequate food supply meant that the cities could not be maintained and so the cities were gradually abandoned.

The latest scholarly thinking is broadly in agreement with this picture, although it makes significant changes to the causal links of the argument. The consensus is that the trigger for the 'Maya collapse' was over- rather than under-population. The Classic Maya civilization was so successful that its population grew beyond

Above: Over-population followed by intensive farming seems to have been the cause of the southern Maya collapse.

Right: In a Bonampak mural the halach uinic *(lord) and lieutenants, standing, watch as prisoners have their nails torn out.*

the point at which the land could support it. The farmers turned to highly intensive methods of cultivation, which disturbed the ecological balance and in time this led to severe environmental damage. Disease may also have contributed. Now the population began to fall, as evidenced in the archaeological record. Rising levels of hunger and fear over future shortages fuelled ever-more violent exchanges between city-states, which competed for the fertile land available. Finally, the area was abandoned.

Throughout the previous centuries, when the Maya cities were locked in almost continuous conflict, there had been few changes in the boundaries of the city-states. Wars were conducted in large part in search of royal or noble captives for sacrifice and for common soldiers to be sold as slaves. But there is evidence from the last of the carved stelae (see box) that in the final years, lowland Maya cities were seeking to expand in an entirely new way, fighting for land more than for honour.

The modern scholarly argument therefore suggests that intensifying war between the city-states was a symptom rather than a cause of the collapse of the southern Maya region. The Maya fought themselves to a standstill as they competed for land   and perhaps also sought to capture armies of prisoners in order to mount lavish sacrifices that might be enough to bring back times of plenty.

CHAPTER FIVE

ROYAL POWER, LAW AND ORDER

In the Maya city of Palenque, in northern Chiapas, three temple-pyramids known to archaeologists as the Temple of the Cross, the Temple of the Foliated Cross and the Temple of the Sun contain stone panels carved with images and hieroglyphic inscriptions that establish an ancestral line for the dynasty of Palenque's most celebrated ruler, Lord Pacal. The images present the royal ruler as a link to the realm of the gods and ancestors, as the guarantor of fertility, rain and crops, and as a warrior, powerful in battle. These were the three key roles performed by the Maya ruler to justify his pre-eminent position.

The Aztec *tlatoani*, or ruler of each city-state, was understood to be both a promoter of fertility and a great warrior prince. His ritual names included *inan, ita altepetl* ('Mother and Father of the City') and he took the role of rainbringer in an important fertility ceremony conducted each year on Mount Tláloc. He was essentially the chief priest, conducting certain sacrificial rites himself, and was understood to assume divine power during his complex coronation rites. The power of the gods burned in him and was refreshed from time to time in ritual sacrifices. He was the living image of the warrior god Huitzilopochtli and the army's commander-in-chief. As part of the coronation rituals he had to conduct a military campaign to celebrate his divinely ordained election to the post.

Left: At Palenque, city of King Pacal, a wooded hill looms behind the raised Temple of the Foliated Cross (left).

STRUCTURES OF POWER

The rulers of Classic Period Maya states were dynastic leaders revered by their people as 'holy kings'. A man such as King Chan Muwan of Bonampak held sway, from a canopied throne protected by a curtain and sometimes covered with jaguar skins, over a large palace retinue that included his extended family, military staff, kitchen workers, dancers with a band of musicians and the *ak k'u hun* (chief scribe), himself in charge of a team of artists, sculptors and scribes. The important position of *sahal*, head of the military staff, was usually filled by a close relative of the king. A *sahal* could be dispatched to govern a provincial town.

The Spanish conquistadors encountered a similar situation in 16th-century Yucatán. Each state was governed by a ruler known as *halach uinic* ('true man'), who governed with the support of a council that was doubtless appointed

Left: A cylindrical vessel left in a tomb in the Maya city of Tikal represents a splendidly attired lord receiving a visitor.

from his blood relatives. He lived in great splendour in the state's main city at the head of an impressive retinue, receiving the highly prized cacao and other produce from the lands he governed and setting himself apart by the magnificence of his appearance and many layers of ritual. Like the Aztec *tlatoani*, the *halach uinic* was viewed in a paternal light; the Spaniards said he was 'father' and 'lord' of the city. He appointed officials known as batabs whose job was to govern provincial towns, with the support of a council. Batabs were magistrates and war leaders as well as administrators.

The Maya ruler took one legitimate wife, but also kept concubines. His wife was greatly revered and, on the evidence of the Bonampak murals, she cut a truly magnificent figure. She is depicted at Bonampak as wearing a necklace and earrings, with swirling hair tied up and a red stole on her arm, setting off the fine white dress that she wears.

STONE RECORDS

In the Classic Period, the holy kings of Maya cities such as Piedras Negras, Tikal, Yaxchilán, Quiriguá and Palenque erected inscribed stelae, thrones, wall panels,

Left: One of the kings of Copán adorns the lid of a ceramic vase left as a mortuary offering c.AD650–800.

door lintels and other monuments recording their accession and its major anniversaries, together with the duration and major military triumphs of their reign and significant ritual sacrifices. At Piedras Negras, for example, each king appears to have set up a monument celebrating his accession on its fifth anniversary. The inscriptions record the anniversary, the date the ruler came to the throne and an earlier date that scholars suggest may be his date of birth or the date on which he was named. The ruler then set up new monuments every five years for as long as his reign lasted. These monuments were carved with an 'accession motif', identified by Tatiana Proskouriakoff. It shows a figure seated on a throne at the top of a ladder, with footsteps visible on a mat over the ladder, indicating the ruler had climbed to his position of royal pre-eminence.

MODES OF SUCCESSION

In the Classic Period, royal power was almost always inherited from father to son, but there is evidence that the line could pass through the daughter in some instances. At Tikal, the daughter of King Kan Boar was given a remarkably rich burial that included valuable imported oyster shell and the skeleton of a spider monkey. Kan Boar's daughter, who is known to archaeologists as 'the Lady of Tikal', is shown on a lintel standing at the right hand of her husband, who succeeded her father as king.

The evidence suggests that a woman could succeed her father in the royal palace only as a wife. Her husband would be 'adopted' by her father and become the rightful heir in her place. Their children would then inherit the throne. In some cases, the son of a royal marriage was not considered fit to rule and power might be passed to his brother, or, if no male member of the immediate family was available, to a more distant relative from the ruling council.

Among the Aztecs, succession was not hereditary. An election was held among the nobles of the highest ranks to determine who should succeed the *tlatoani* and the new ruler was then blessed, following complex coronation rites, by the high priest. However, the election was essentially token. The old

Above: This shell, delicately carved with the prominent nose and features of a Maya nobleman, was worn as a pendant.

ruler would nominate a successor and it would usually have been clear who this would be, for the ruler-in-waiting generally filled the role of *tlaccatecatl* on the elite military council. The appointment was then approved by the nobles' council, although sometimes the leaders of Texcoco and Tlacopán were asked for their input. The successor generally came from among the ruler's close blood relatives. At Tenochtitlán, three grandsons of Moctezuma I Ilhuicamina took power in turn; Axayácatl, Tizoc and Ahuítzotl. In Texcoco, sons usually succeeded fathers.

Left: Moctezuma II prepares for coronation as tlatoani *in an illustration from the* Codex Durán *(1579–81).*

THE POWER OF APPEARANCE

Both Maya kings and Aztec rulers dressed in great splendour as a mark of status and to associate themselves with the gods whose authority they claimed.

THE COSTUME OF KINGS

Classic Period Maya kings wore racks on their backs to support large headdress frames that sometimes rose a metre or more above the brow. The rack and the headdress frame, both made of wood, were covered with elaborate decorative designs which used shells, carved jade,

MAYA KINGSHIP

The magnificent appearance of the Young Maize God in ceramic and other imagery made him a fitting representative of Maya kingship.

The Young Maize God, mythical father of the Hero Twins Hunahpú and Xbalanqué, was patron deity of scribes, as well as a divine embodiment of Maya royalty. He is depicted with splendid jewellery, a royal headdress and a long, tonsured head whose shape represents that of an ear of maize. Sometimes, his fine headdress contains an image of a jester god. On ceramics, the Young Maize God is often shown twice or as one of a pair of twins, reflecting the fact that the father of the Hero Twins, One Hunahpú, descended to Xibalba with his twin brother Seven Hunahpú to play the ball game with the gods of that frightful place. Scholars can only speculate why the Young Maize God should be a patron of scribes. They point to the fact that the paper used for Maya books was made by soaking bark in the same way that maize was treated to make dough, usually using the same water that had been used for the maize.

feathers and textiles. The long, bright-green plumes of the quetzal bird were the most highly prized. The headdress often contained the mask of the rain god Chac or the sun god Ahau Kin.

Some kings wore the stick bundles of the scribe in their headdress, indicating both the high status of the scribe and the fact that the king was literate. The king wore his hair long and wove jewellery and ornaments into it. He built his nose up into a great beak, using putty, wore large ornaments in the enlarged lobes of his ears and had his teeth filed and inlays of jade added.

The king dressed in specific and different costumes when performing his various roles as priest, war leader and civil ruler. In each case, the king carried a symbol of his authority. Along with leading nobles, the king wore a ceremonial version of the costume worn by players of the ball game. This must have been donned for rites associated with the game.

Below: Scholars identify this figure from a Maya vase as a palace dignitary attendant on the king.

Left: A late Classic Period terracotta figure of a Maya warrior has a deer headdress and facial tattoos.

New World, and it is now held by the Museum für Völkerkunde, Vienna. Scholars believe that this particular headdress, which contains 450 quetzal feathers, was worn by priests, possibly when representing Quetzalcóatl himself in temple rites.

Below: A late Classic Period figurine represents a Maya king as both a warrior, with a shield, and a ball player, with a padded protective belt. He is also associated with the rain god Chac.

Above: The decoration on a cylindrical vase grave offering from Tikal depicts a noble with elongated earlobes and large earrings.

Maya kings also appear to have played the ball game, and carvings survive showing kings in the protective costumes worn for the game. A stone panel from La Amelia, Guatemala, depicts the King of Dos Pilas performing a dance of triumph or ritual importance in his game clothes, with a belt and kneepads.

SYMBOLS OF AUTHORITY

In Aztec lands, only the *tlatoani* was permitted to wear the *xicolli*, a decorated waistcoat, and Aztec rulers marked their status by wearing rich jewellery and ornaments made of rock-crystal and jade. The plumes of the quetzal were also used as a symbol of kingly authority. The quetzal was understood to be an important *nahualli* or animal form of the god Quetzalcóatl, the Plumed Serpent who was identified with the wise ruler and high priest of Tollán, Topiltzin. Aztec rulers wore green quetzal feathers or green stones as a mark of sovereignty. When Moctezuma II sent an offering of gifts to Hernán Cortés shortly after the Spaniards landed in April 1519, he included a headdress of green feathers. Cortés sent it on to his lord, Charles V, in a consignment of treasures from the

CORONATION SPECTACLE

The power of the ruler in both Maya and Aztec realms was often expressed through public ceremony. The vast temple rituals that culminated in human sacrifices impressed not only the rulers' subjects but also outsiders, including both allies and enemies.

VISIBLE MIGHT
The Aztecs required the lords of some allied states to live in Tenochtitlán. Here they witnessed spectacular demonstrations of Aztec might and authority on the steps

Left: The splendour of Maya royal ceremony is celebrated in this image on a polychrome vase buried at Uaxactún near Tikal.

and at the summit of the Great Pyramid. Ahuítzotl's rededication of the Great Temple in 1487, in which as many as 80,000 victims may have been sacrificed, was a dramatic expression of his power as recently installed *tlatoani* and of the Aztecs' pre-eminence, as well as of his people's devotion to their gods.

Another public statement of the Aztec ruler's might was his complex coronation ceremony. In Tenochtitlán, the council's approval of the appointment of a new ruler was the start of a prolonged coronation ceremony, a powerful religious drama of several days' duration in which the whole state took part.

RETREAT
The rites began with a sober period of retreat. Following the death of the previous *tlatoani*, his elected successor was publicly stripped of all finery and symbols of status. Before the Great Pyramid in the centre of Tenochtitlán, he stood before the silent crowd dressed only in a loincloth, before being led by the rulers of the allied cities Texcoco and Tlacopán up the steep side of the pyramid to the shrine of the god Huitzilopochtli. There he was given a robe of dark green marked

with the image of skulls. He burned incense in honour of the god. Afterwards, he descended the pyramid with a company of nobles and began a retreat lasting four days and nights in the military headquarters (*tlacochcalco*) within the ceremonial precinct. Every 12 hours, at noon and midnight, he climbed once more to the shrine of Huitzilopochtli and made offerings of his own blood, pricked from his ears, lower legs or arms.

ROBING AND ENTHRONEMENT
Following the sombre retreat, the second stage, a magnificent robing and enthronement, was full of colour. The new ruler and the company of penitent nobles processed from the *tlacochcalco* to one of the city's great palaces. The *tlatoani* of Texcoco dressed the new ruler in a robe of shining fabric with a glistening waistband, solemnly placed a greenstone crown on his head and adorned him with fabulous jewellery, including emerald earrings and nosepiece, gold armbands and anklets, and jaguar-skin sandals. He led him to a splendid throne covered with jaguar skins and eagle feathers.

This enthronement was followed by a public ceremony. The new ruler was carried on a litter to the Great Pyramid, where, before the sacred shrine of Huitzilopochtli, he used jaguar claws to let his own blood for a sacrificial offering and made a sacrifice of quails. He was then taken to a place containing either a sunstone or an eagle vessel, according to differing accounts, to make further blood sacrifices in honour of the sun.

Next, the new ruler made a stately progress, still carried on his litter, to the *coateocalli*, the building within the ritual enclosure where the Aztecs kept the captured gods of conquered peoples, some of which were accepted into the Aztec pantheon. Here he made further offerings of his blood to signify his devotion to the religious calendar, before proceeding to an earth temple used in spring planting

and other agricultural festivals. He made offerings to the sacred earth, validating his succession as ruler of the land.

The public ceremonial of enthronement was concluded when the king returned to the palace in the company of leading nobles for a series of speeches. He was informed that he was now greater than his fellow men, for his sacred role as leader gave him the power to speak to the gods and made him the deities' embodiment on Earth. The divinities filled him and were within him, they were his eyes, his tongue, his ears; symbolically, they were his claws and his sharp jaguar teeth.

BLESSED BY THE GODS
The new ruler now called on his people to follow him to war, for the next stage of his coronation ceremony required that he lead a military campaign to prove that the gods blessed him in battle. When Moctezuma I Ilhuicamina's grandson Tizoc led a dismal failure of a coronation campaign to Metztitlán following his accession in 1481, the people saw his poor performance in the field as a very bad omen for the reign that he had been seeking to celebrate. However, the campaign was judged a success and a propitious omen when the new ruler returned laden with booty and leading ranks of prisoners for sacrifice. This was the judgement made of Tizoc's successor, his brother Ahuítzotl, upon his return from his coronation campaign.

CONFIRMATION
The final stage of the sequence of rituals was a great public celebration known as confirmation, in which allies and even enemy states were expected to send offerings of tribute and the new *tlatoani* gave feasts in Tenochtitlán. On the first day, the new ruler made public demonstration of the primacy of Tenochtitlán within the Triple Alliance, when he presented the leaders of Texcoco and Tlacopán with their symbols of status. Afterwards, the allied rulers led a 2,000-strong company of nobles and warriors in a stately dance.

Above: Elite warriors donned ceremonial finery including feathered helmets and decorated armour for the coronation.

The new ruler of Tenochtitlán then made a triumphant entrance wearing a magnificent costume adorned with quetzal feathers and laden with jewellery, and the dancing group made a circle around him. He made a formal presentation of the insignia of office to the gathered ranks of Aztec society, so that his authority and pre-eminent status were clear to all. The ceremony had a bloody ending in a vast public sacrifice of the prisoners brought back from the coronation campaign.

The ritual coronation was a means of reaffirming and celebrating the many aspects of the Aztec ruler's greatness as the chief figure of the leading city of the mighty Aztec empire.

Below: Members of the Aztec nobility and imperial bureaucracy received official recognition of their status from the new tlatoani *in a palace ceremony.*

SUN KING: THE GLORY OF KING PACAL

The greatness of King Pacal of Palenque can be judged from his magnificent funerary crypt, rich grave offerings and towering sepulchral monument, the Temple of the Inscriptions, which stands atop a 20m (65ft) stepped pyramid. His city-state, Palenque, stands in a striking position, beneath a line of hills thick with rainforest, at the edge of the Usumacinta River floodplain, looking toward the Gulf of Mexico.

SPLENDOUR IN DEATH

The crypt, accessed by a long stairway leading downwards from the Temple of the Inscriptions, lies some 24m (80ft) below the temple floor. Within the crypt, the king's body was laid in a sarcophagus of red-painted stone, wearing a collar of precious jade, a green headband, several jade necklaces and mother-of-pearl and jade earpieces. Over his face was a lifelike mask fashioned from jade, obsidian and shells. The outside of the sarcophagus was carved with images of the king's ancestors, while nine stucco figures around the walls of the crypt represented the main gods of the underworld. In the corridors of the Temple of the Inscriptions

Right: Pacal's jade mosaic funeral mask has eyes of shell, mother of pearl and obsidian. A T-shaped amulet provides magical protection for the mouth.

were stone slabs carved with lists of kings. From these, together with accompanying lists commissioned by Pacal's son Chan-Bahlum, scholars have been able to construct a succession of 12 rulers. Together with the list from Copán, these are among the most detailed and complete dynastic lists of any ruling family in the Maya realm.

WHO WAS HE?

The remarkable King Pacal reigned at Palenque for 68 years. From carvings in the temple and an inscription that runs along the edge of the lid of his sarcophagus, we know that he was born on 24 March in AD603, acceded to the throne on 27 July AD615 and died, aged 81, on 29 September AD684. Scholars have identified his name, which is written both with the image of a small warshield and the hieroglyphs that made the sounds *pa*, *ca* and *la* – spelling *pacal*, which was the word for 'shield'. His full name was K'inich Janaa' Pakal ('Lord Great Sun Shield').

King Pacal is also a most unusual ruler in that the king apparently inherited the throne through his mother's line rather than by the more usual patrilineal descent, as was expected among the Maya. His mother, Lady Zac-Kuk, was ruler herself for a period. Pacal inherited the throne in her name when he

Above: This Palenque relief depicts the ceremony transferring power from Lady Zac-Kuk to her 12-year-old son Pacal.

was 12, but she lived for a further 25 years and may have been the power behind the throne. Only after she died in AD640 did Pacal begin to have significant inscriptions carved to justify his rule.

In Pacal's reign, Palenque became the dominant city in the region. As its ruler, Pacal controlled a large area: Palenque made marriage and other alliances with Tikal, Pomoná and Tortuguero. The city appears to have been at war with Toniná, for in the 8th century, a king of Toniná captured Kan Xul, one of Pacal's sons.

LEARNING FROM BURIAL RITES

The details of Pacal's burial rites show that both he and his subjects expected the deceased ruler to live on as a god after his death. When the great king was buried, five of his subjects were sacrificed so that they could accompany him on his journey to the underworld. The burial also shows that Pacal claimed authority

Above: Palenque's Temple of the Count pyramid (right) commands a view of the Temple of the Inscriptions (upper left).

for his dynasty by associating his ancestors and descendants with the sun god. The lid of his sarcophagus, which shows him descending the length of the world tree to the underworld, also depicts the sun moving between death and life. At his side within the sarcophagus was a jade figure of the sun god, suggesting that the king would rise again into the eastern sky after his underworld trials. The royal succession from Pacal to his descendants was symbolically blessed by the sun.

PASSING ON ROYAL POWER

Pacal's son, Chan-Bahlum, succeeded his father in AD684. He built the Temples of the Sun, the Cross and the Foliated Cross to celebrate his succession. The relation of this group to the main Temple of the Inscriptions confirms the sun god's approval. Once in every year, at sunset on the winter

solstice, the Maya understood the sun to undergo a symbolic death. The setting sun would shine through a dip in the ridge behind the Temple of the Inscriptions and fall on the carved scenes in the Temple of the Cross that celebrate Pacal passing his

royal power to Chan-Bahlum. As the sun set, its light would travel down the stair to King Pacal's tomb, symbolically entering the underworld with the king, prior to its rebirth the next morning.

Scholars believe that Pacal ordered the construction of the Temple of the Inscriptions as his own mortuary monument when he reached his seventies and understood that he was nearing the close of his long reign. The temple pyramid was completed after Pacal's death by Chan-Bahlum. The discovery of Pacal's tomb by Mexican archaeologist Albert Ruz in 1952 entirely changed the way that scholars view Maya temple pyramids, for it was the first evidence to emerge that some of these great constructions were essentially mortuary monuments.

Left: Pacal's final home, the Temple of the Inscriptions pyramid, has nine levels. Its stairway climbs to a five-bay sanctuary. The secret staircase to Pacal's crypt within the pyramid begins inside the sanctuary.

MOCTEZUMA II IN HIS POMP

Remembered primarily today as the last independent Aztec leader, Moctezuma II is the ruler who was ignominiously captured by the Spaniards and who apparently lost the confidence of his people; the man who lived to see the empire of the Triple Alliance swept away by a small band of invaders like a spider's web in the wind. However, at the time of the Spanish Conquest, the empire was still expanding and apparently healthy.

Below and far right: 17th-century Spanish artists Miguel and Juan Gonzalez show Cortés riding to meet Moctezuma II.

HIERARCHY AND ETIQUETTE

Moctezuma II ruled with great pomp and absolute authority over Tenochtitlán and the Aztec empire. One of his first

Above: This later portrait of Moctezuma II presents a Europeanized view of the last Aztec leader's magnificent appearance.

endeavours, after his coronation war and the celebration of his confirmation rites, was to boost his own status and reinforce the standing of the nobility by introducing new court etiquette. He brought in laws on clothing and behaviour that set the *pipiltin* or nobility apart from the *macehuales* or commoners. For example, he stripped commoner-warriors who had excelled in battle of their much-valued privilege of wearing special clothes and insignia and insisted that they dress like the other members of their caste. He also introduced elaborate court ritual that underlined his own standing as an absolute ruler, the living image of the god Huitzilopochtli.

To further boost his authority, Moctezuma II brought his own men into government and the palace hierarchy. In the inner circle, he removed the officials

THE RAIN MAN

An annual ceremony held on Mount Tláloc cast the *tlatoani* in the role of rainmaker and illustrates how the cult of the Aztec ruler reflected his dual status as a warrior-leader and a fertility lord.

The ceremony was held in April or May, during the dry season, to draw the rain out from within the mountain. The rulers of Tenochtitlán, Texcoco, Tlacopán and Xochimilco made a pilgrimage to a temple high on Mount Tláloc. The temple was roofless, but built with high walls that cut off the view of the surrounding countryside. Within were rocks set out to echo the arrangement of peaks normally visible from the mountaintop, which included the divine mountains Popocatépetl and Ixtaccíhuatl.

The rulers carried gifts for the mountain-gods into the temple, then dressed the rock-idols in magnificent costumes. They left the temple but re-entered with offerings including food and the blood of a male infant. Afterwards, the rulers themselves feasted with their retinue on the open mountaintop.

Scholars interpret the ceremony as an act of fertilization, likening the rock temple to a cave, which the Aztecs understood to be a way into the spiritual world. This mountaintop cave was a place of opposites, where the earth met the sky and the spirit world met the physical world. The rulers' offering, like the large human sacrifices in city temples, was intended to recycle energy within the cosmos.

In the weeks after the ceremony, the dry season would come to an end. The first sign of the change would be rain clouds collecting around the summit of Mount Tláloc.

appointed by his predecessor, Ahuítzotl, and replaced them with his own close relatives and followers. (In some accounts, he ruthlessly had Ahuítzotl's men put to death.) He even removed the servants from the palaces of Tenochtitlán. In a canny move, he brought junior nobles from provincial cities of the empire and put them to work in the palaces. He calculated that the rulers of those cities would not consider revolt while their children were under his control in Tenochtitlán.

When Hernán Cortés and the Spaniards first encountered Moctezuma II at the entrance to Tenochtitlán, the Aztec leader emerged from the city borne on a litter by four noblemen and surrounded by a great number of slaves carrying goods to be offered to the gods. Moctezuma wore golden jewellery, a diadem encrusted with turquoise and the brilliant green feathers of the quetzal bird. He dismounted and walked forward supported by two nobles of the inner circle in a ceremonial manner of walking that showed great respect for the visitor. When Cortés approached to make a gift of Venetian pearls he was prevented from touching the Aztec ruler. After both had made speeches, Moctezuma led the visitors into a temple where he called on the god Huitzilopochtli, calling him his 'father', and received offerings from the rulers of Tacuba and Texcoco. At one point Moctezuma, the living embodiment of the Aztecs' principal god, lifted his clothes to show Cortés his arms and torso, saying, 'Look, I am only flesh and blood, like you'.

Moctezuma's quasi-divine standing played a significant part both in his own downfall and in that of the Aztec empire. His capture by the Spaniards was only possible because the Aztecs could not imagine that anyone would dare to manhandle this imperial figure and hold him to ransom. A Spanish delegation led by Cortés merely asked for an audience,

Above: Moctezuma II approaches his fateful first meeting with Cortés, carried out from Tenochtitlán in great style on a litter.

claiming that they wanted to complain of a supposed Aztec plan for a military action against the Spanish garrison at Veracruz. They were admitted and, finding no precautions to safeguard the emperor's person, seized him. Moctezuma had to cooperate, for his own survival. In captivity, and pleading for the Aztecs not to attack the Spanish compound, Moctezuma found that his authority was melting away.

On a larger scale, the Spaniards benefited from the fact that so much power was concentrated in one man. By eliminating him, they created a power vacuum that they were able to exploit to their advantage. The conquistadors certainly found that among the Maya, where there was no single figure to be eliminated at a stroke, conquest was a more difficult and challenging undertaking.

WISE GOVERNANCE, STRICT PUNISHMENT

The rulers of the Triple Alliance developed a legal code that defined the punishments for a range of misdemeanours and crimes, as well as set solutions for particular types of dispute. The code was used as a unifying factor and was strictly applied throughout the empire, without allowance for local differences or the details of a case.

THE BASIS OF THE LEGAL CODE

Scholars are unsure whether the code was based on ancient Mesoamerican tradition, as Netzahualcóyotl of Texcoco claimed, or whether it was developed specifically to deal with the difficulties of keeping law and order across the empire, with its many different terrains and complex mix of urban and rural peoples. The code was certainly a valued tool of central control, for it eliminated the risk of provincial lords undermining Aztec authority by developing their own legal system or list of punishments.

SON OF THE GODS

The Aztec legal system is said to have been devised by Netzahualcóyotl, the remarkable ruler of Texcoco who as a youth witnessed the killing of his father Ixtlilxóchitl and fled into exile before returning many years later to take power in the city of his birth.

Netzahualcóyotl was both a skilled politician and also a brilliant ruler who presided over his city for 41 years (1431–72) and won a glittering reputation for himself as a builder, poet, philosopher and legislator.

In part, perhaps, because of the dramatic events of his youth, an aura built around him and his life became enshrouded in myth. The story was told that he was son of the gods themselves, and that he would never taste death.

The chronicler Fernando de Alva Ixtlilxóchitl even suggested that Netzahualcóyotl had an understanding of divine reality that went far beyond that of his contemporaries, grasping the possibility of a single supreme creator deity rather than a multiplicity of many-faceted gods. He was the *tlatoani* who built a temple to an abstract god named Tloquenahuaque ('The One Who is Always Near').

Part of Netzahualcóyotl's brilliance may have lain in the fact that he constructed this godlike image for himself. He lent authority to the legal system he created by claiming to have revived the laws of Quetzalcóatl-Topiltzin, wise and fair ruler of Tula, in days of yore.

Aztecs were generally agreed as to what constituted good behaviour. According to Bernardino de Sahagún, author of *General History of the Things of New Spain*, virtuous Aztecs were obedient and honest, treating their fellows with respect and showing discretion in their dealings with others. Virtuous men and women worked hard, whether in the fields, at their sewing, preparing food, in an artisan's workshop, or in the marketplace. They brought energy to their work, without overindulging in sleep but rising early and labouring for long hours. They ate and drank in moderation; drunkenness was particularly frowned upon. They did not make a great noise when eating, thought carefully before speaking and were circumspect in what they said. They dressed and behaved with modesty. Children were raised to understand and follow this code.

Left: Although drunkenness was not encouraged, large amounts of pulque *were drunk during religious festivals.*

Below: A bronze image of Netzahualcóyotl seeks to capture his character as wise governor and deliverer of laws.

Above: A Florentine Codex *image shows judgement passed and punishment meted out under the Aztec law and order system.*

The *Codex Mendoza* contains a visual record of the trial and execution of the Mixtec leader of Coixtlahuaca, whose people attacked some Aztec merchants. This event was used by Moctezuma I Ilhuicamina as the pretext for a war that brought the Mixtecs to their knees and resulted in the payment of rich tribute into Aztec coffers. The codex image shows the merchants being killed and the arrival of Aztec emissaries to administer justice. They deliver a symbolic headdress, which indicates that the chief faces severe punishment. One of their number delivers a judgement on the ruler, who is put to death by strangulation while his child and principal wife are tied up roughly with slave collars around their necks.

The Mapa Quinatzin depicts legal process in Texcoco, whose ruler Netzahualcóyotl was famed as a legislator. A provincial chieftain who has had the temerity to rebel is warned, like the ruler of Coixtlahuaca, by being presented with a symbolic headdress. Then he is executed. Judges are depicted being put to death by strangulation because they have failed to follow required procedures and heard cases in their private lodgings.

PUNISHMENT

Punishments for wrongdoers included jailing and execution by strangulation, at the stake, or stoning. Theft was punished by strangulation. Drunks were strictly punished, with a sliding scale of penalties. The alcoholic drink *pulque* was only allowed for nobles, those who were sick and those aged over 52 years, although warriors could win the right to drink *pulque* as a reward for great bravery in battle. Those found drunk would have their heads shaved on the first occasion, on the second they would suffer the additional penalty of having their house knocked down. People found drunk on a third occasion would be put to death.

Right: Among the Aztecs, the rabbit was associated with the strong alcoholic drink pulque *and with drunkenness.*

THE MAYA LAW CODE

The Maya imposed severe penalties on those people who threatened social cohesion by committing crimes such as murder or adultery.

DIVINE PLAN

The Maya did not accept that bad things could happen by accident, for they viewed every event as the fulfilment of patterns that could be read in the stars and perhaps in the past, and which were set in motion by the gods. A hunter who killed another man by accident in the forest was just as guilty of murder as a man who killed another before witnesses in a quarrel over food. The unfortunate hunter must have been chosen by the gods to meet this end. Similarly, a person who lost or damaged someone else's belongings by accident was treated as if he or she had done it with intent and was required to compensate the unfortunate victim. Those who had no wealth of their own with which to pay compensation,

Above: Punishments for adultery were very severe and the man was executed. This clay couple was found in a Jaina Island grave.

nor wealthy relatives to provide help, faced slavery. They would be freed once they had worked off the money they owed to the victim.

PUNISHMENT

The punishment for murder was death. According to Bishop Diego de Landa, the murderer was placed in stocks and put to death by the relatives of the person he had killed. It appears that killing an animal for no reason was seen as akin to murder and the perpetrator might be severely disciplined for having brought shame on his patrilineal or matrilineal social group. Maya hunters were very serious about their responsibility to respect the animals on which they relied. They

Left: The figure on this Maya vase appears to be giving instruction or delivering a judgement on a question of law.

Right: Royal anniversaries were a time of clemency. A king of Copán wears a headdress celebrating the rain god Chac.

would make ritual atonement after killing an animal by sprinkling blood drawn from the penis or tongue on to a part of the creature.

When couples were caught committing adultery, the man was punished with death. If the couple were caught *in flagrante*, the man would be taken from the bed and bound hand and foot, humiliated and dragged before the judges. After hearing the case and declaring his guilt, the victim would be handed to the husband, who was permitted to exact revenge by taking the other's life. The usual method of execution, or so Bishop de Landa reports, was to crush the adulterer's head by dropping a heavy rock on it from a height.

Theft was also considered a serious offence. The Maya did not add doors to their houses, so that there was no way of barring entry to passers-by; many people hung a bell-string in the doorway that would sound when someone entered and alert whoever was at home. A person caught stealing would be thrown into slavery. He would often be given a set period of time in which to work off the cost of his crime, after which he could return to free society. However, if the members of his patriarchal or matriarchal social group were wealthy, they would pay compensation to the person he stole from and he would be free to go.

The Maya did not put thieves, murderers or adulterers in jail. The only people they kept in captivity were the captives they brought home in triumph from war who were kept for sacrifice on festival days or at the celebration of a king's anniversary. These victims-in-waiting were treated with respect until the time for sacrifice came, when they might be subjected to severe physical indignities in the name of the ancestor-gods.

Below: Maya merchants traded near and far. This Preclassic vase (c.900–200BC) is from the Sula Valley, Honduras.

TRADE AND ENFORCEMENT

Maya merchants were a privileged class known as *ppolms*, some trading by sea in great fleets of canoes, others carrying goods along trails and roadways.

A merchant god, Ek Chuah, presided over the transactions of the land traders. It was a religious duty to act with honour, but such was the wealth involved in large transactions for precious cargoes of cacao or greenstones that sometimes greed got the better of individuals and sharp practice crept in.

Maya merchants did not make written deals. Instead, they would come to a verbal agreement, which was usually signalled by drinking a toast in public. These deals were then considered binding. If a merchant refused to honour the terms of a deal, his deceit might be considered justification enough to launch a war. The end result might be wealth far greater than that involved in the deal in the form of booty, slaves and tribute.

However, while sometimes a cause of war, Maya trade may have been a source of peace in one important respect. The success of Maya merchants may have saved their people from attack by the land-hungry armies of the Aztec empire. The Maya traded regularly with the peoples of the Triple Alliance, exchanging salt, cacao beans and the highly prized green plumes of the quetzal bird for ornaments and tools in copper. The success of these trading links perhaps served to deter the Aztecs from launching military campaigns in Yucatán.

CLANS AND POWER: MAYA SOCIAL GROUPS

Each Maya belonged to two blood groups: the matrilineal group, descended from the mother, and the patrilineal group, descended from the father. Each individual had both a name given by and inherited from the mother and another taken from the father.

PATRIMONY

Property could only be inherited from the father. Like the king's crown, belongings only passed down the patrilineal line. Members of a patrilineal group were expected to help one another in times of need. For example, they would buy out a relative who had been thrown into slavery because of debt or crime. The patrilineal group also held lands in common.

According to Bishop de Landa, each family among the common people was allocated 37sq m (400sq ft) of land to farm. This unit of land was known as a *hun uinic*. Scholars believe the matrilineal and patrilineal groupings were also used

Below: The 'Nunnery' at Uxmal may have been occupied by members of one social class or worshippers of a particular god.

to control marriage between relatives. For example, a man might marry his mother's brother's daughter or his father's sister's daughter, but he would be barred from making other particular marriages.

CLASS DIVISIONS

Alongside and cutting across these blood groupings there were strong class divisions. It was extremely prestigious to be able to trace your lineage on both your mother's and father's side back across many generations to a noble family. Indeed, the word for a noble, *almehen*, translates as 'a man whose bloodline can be read on both sides'. Among members of the nobility were wealthy farmers who owned their own land, prosperous merchants, priests, leading warriors and priests. All those who held office within the political hierarchy, including councillors, judges and governors, were members of the nobility. The most important positions were filled by close members of the ruler's own blood group. The chiefs were carried in a litter decorated with plumes and borne on the shoulders of strong men.

Above: Members of the Maya nobility refashioned their looks by using clay to join the bridge of the nose to the forehead.

Scribes also occupied an elevated social position. They were leading members of the king's retinue. Most cities probably had a school for scribes, where royal and noble children such as the younger sons and daughters of the king or his children by secondary wives and concubines would learn the complex skills of reading and writing Maya hieroglyphs.

LITERACY AND CLASS

Literacy was probably not widespread among the general population. Scholars estimate that perhaps one in four of the Maya could read, and probably far fewer could write. Archaeologists have found attempts at writing by non-elite scribes at minor settlements or on the bricks that were fired at Comacalco, but these are

not comprehensible because those responsible had clearly not mastered the difficult technique required. All they could manage was a crude imitation of the fine calligraphy found on carvings and ceramics produced by the elite scribes.

Beneath the nobility were the free workers, those who were allotted the *hun uinic* on which to grow their maize. They were liable to pay taxes in the form of crops to a tax collector. The priests who played such a vital role in reading the stars and patterns of history to determine the correct planting times were supported with crops from the field. The farmers probably saw the food sent to the temple as a gift to the gods, eaten by the priesthood on their behalf.

SLAVES

Some of the men worked the lands on behalf of the wealthy. There was also a large class of slaves. Many were men and women captured in war for, in general, only the more noble among the captives were sacrificed while the poorer prisoners were put into slavery. Others were individuals from Maya homelands who had been brought to slavery by wrongdoing or by poverty. Slaves were also traded across the vast network of routes that crisscrossed the Maya lands. For most, there was no way out of their condition and their children also would be slaves, although it was possible to buy individuals out of slavery.

Female slaves worked drawing water from wells, dyeing cloth and grinding maize. Male slaves were put to work as labourers, fishermen and carriers of cargo for merchants. The males were given an ill-kempt appearance, with ragged clothing and roughly cut short hair.

Maya architecture and city planning reflected and reinforced these class divisions. In general, the king, his retinue and the nobility lived close to the centre of the city. The Maya city was usually centred on the temple complex and its fine plazas. Around this were grouped the palaces and homes of the elite nobles, with the merchants and other professionals living in smaller dwellings beyond them and the humble homes of the working people more distant still.

Above: Maya rulers are regularly modelled or depicted on vases occupying the throne that symbolizes their power.

Left: In the Maya social pyramid, the king at the highest point was raised far above the workers of the land and slaves at the lowest level.

THE MANY LEVELS OF AZTEC SOCIETY

Aztec society was highly stratified. The most important division was between the *pipiltin*, or nobles, and the *macehuales* or commoners. These two social groups were essentially castes; there was no possibility of a man of humble birth rising to join the nobility. A boy's destiny was determined not just by his date of birth in the ritual calendar, but also by his caste. To be born on the date 1-Alligator was a good omen: the priests promised that a noble's son born on this day could expect to become a wealthy ruler of men. The

Below: An image from the Florentine Codex *shows an Aztec metalworker making objects of gold for the wealthiest of the nobility.*

best they could promise a farmer's son born on the same day, however, was that he might become a valiant warrior in the service of the city-state.

THE NOBILITY

Nobles often received income from land holdings. They had access to prestigious positions in the priesthood and in the highest ranks of the army. Some served in the civil administration as provincial governors and judges, ambassadors and tax-collectors. Those of the highest rank were advisers to the *tlatoani*. Other nobles of lesser standing might become scribes and teachers. They had many privileges. The men were

Left: Gazing upwards, this life-size clay figure may represent a learned astronomer-priest.

allowed to take several wives and build houses of two storeys. They sent their children to *calmecac* or priestly schools. Here they learned to read and write, and to study the ritual calendar and its meaning. They also learned battlefield strategy, history and mythology, and practised martial arts.

THE COMMONERS

Commoners were primarily farmers, fishermen and soldiers. Members of the tribal clan or *calpulli* held land in common and most farmers worked the land or water owned by their clan grouping. They were liable to pay tax to the *tlatoani* and could be called on to serve in the army or to work on construction projects. If a man neglected his area or died without having children, the clan would reassign that particular piece of land to another member of the blood grouping. Another type of farmer, known as *mayeque*, worked land owned by nobles.

Soldiers had the best chance of rising through the social ranks. There were many rewards for bravery in battle, including social privileges. But there was no way into the highest positions in the army, which were reserved for members of the nobility.

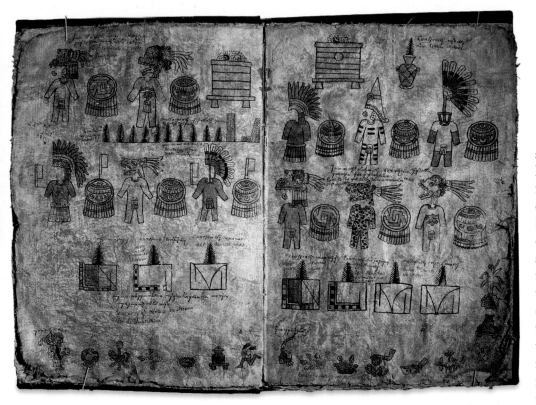

Above: Some of the many Aztec styles of clothing, headdresses and jewellery are detailed in the Codex Mendoza *(c.1541).*

As the empire grew, divisions in Aztec society blurred and private ownership of land increased. When Tenochtitlán was founded, most land was held by tribal clans or *calpulli*. By the time of the Spanish Conquest, there were two types of landholding nobles. At the highest level stood a small group of nobles of ancient families directly related to the *tlatoani*, who owned territories that were worked on their behalf by farmers legally tied to the soil. At a lower level were warriors who had gained land as a reward for military achievement. These awards were normally for one generation, but in practice warriors tended to be allowed to leave land to their offspring. For this reason, Moctezuma II reinforced the distinction between nobility and commoners. He enforced strict laws on the dress code permitted for the castes and introduced ceremonial procedures that further set nobility apart.

Some men and women became slaves. People could volunteer for slavery if they were destitute and could become free again if circumstances improved; perhaps if clan members aided them. The children of slaves were not considered slaves.

ARTISANS

Some commoners achieved a measure of wealth by working as professional merchants (*pochteca*) or as artisans. Both groups lived in their own quarters in Aztec cities. Merchants were usually their own masters: they travelled widely throughout the empire, some trading on behalf of the ruler as well as carrying their own goods. They brought to the Aztec lands many of the raw materials such as precious metals and quetzal feathers needed by the artisans in their work. Some were secret agents, used to spy on allies and enemies and to listen out for whispers of impending revolts and other trouble. If prominent merchants were attacked or killed abroad, the *tlatoani* was quick to send the army to exact retribution. The Aztecs had a very high regard for the work of the skilled artisans who produced precious jewellery, feathered

headdresses, fine costumes and stone ornaments. They honoured their craftsmen with the name *tolteca*, a reference to the ancient Toltecs whom the Aztecs revered. Some artisans were employed by individual nobles but others were free agents, producing artefacts as required. The more successful merchants and artisans became wealthy but they could never cross the caste line to become members of the nobility.

Below: This illustration from the Codex Mendoza *(c.1541) presents the stages in the career of an Aztec imperial officer.*

CHAPTER SIX

PAST, PRESENT AND FUTURE

Mesoamericans did not understand time to be an orderly procession from the past to the future, from the beginnings of the world to its end. For one thing, they believed time to be cyclical. The Aztecs, for example, believed that we live in the Fifth Sun or 'age' and that our age would be brought to a sudden end, as had its predecessors. They also believed that time was sacred, charged with the power of the gods. Its movements could be fluid and unpredictable as the gods chose. Mesoamerican deities could take many forms simultaneously and one of these forms was time itself. In any moment there were divine influences at work for good and bad and the people relied on priestly diviners to interpret time.

A 52-year time span was produced by the intersection of the two calendars used by the Aztecs and their Mesoamerican cousins. Mesoamericans separated by centuries and by miles – perhaps from as early as the Olmec civilization in the first millennium BC to the Maya and Aztecs at the time of the Conquest, and from the Teotihuacanos in the north to the inhabitants of Copán in the south-east – used a 365-day solar calendar to plot religious festivals alongside a 260-day calendar for divining the future. The first day of the 365-day calendar and the first day of the 260-day calendar intersected only once every 52 years. The Aztecs called this time span a 'bundle of years' while the Maya version is usually 'the Calendar Round'.

Left: Hunting god Mixcóatl slays a feline predator. In one Aztec creation myth, Mixcóatl hunted down earth goddess Cihuacóatl for love. Their union produced Quetzalcóatl, the great Plumed Serpent himself, bringer of winds and light.

STARTING FROM ZERO: MATHEMATICS

The Maya used a sophisticated mathematical notation that enabled them to write very large numbers in their carved inscriptions and in codices. They were among the first peoples – along with the ancient Babylonians, the Chinese and the Hindus of India – to develop the concept of zero and a symbol for it. Among the Maya, zero was represented not by an empty circle (0), but by a stylized image of a shell.

DOTS AND BARS

The Maya did not have the familiar decimal system, based on 10, but instead a count based on 20 (called a vigesimal system). Scholars suggest that the unit of 20 may have been used because it matches the number of fingers and toes in the human body. The Maya scribes and craftsmen wrote the numbers 1 to 4 with simple dots. One dot meant 1, two dots 2 and so on. The number 5 was written with a horizontal bar, and 6 was a single bar with a dot above it. They were able to write numbers up to 19 with a combination of horizontal bars and dots. For example, 17 was written with three bars, making 15, and two dots.

To write larger numbers they used these same symbols arranged in vertical columns. The bottom line showed units (1 to 19), the line above it numbers of twenties, the line above it numbers

Below: This detail from the Postclassic Madrid Codex *shows the bar and dot symbols used by the Maya in counting.*

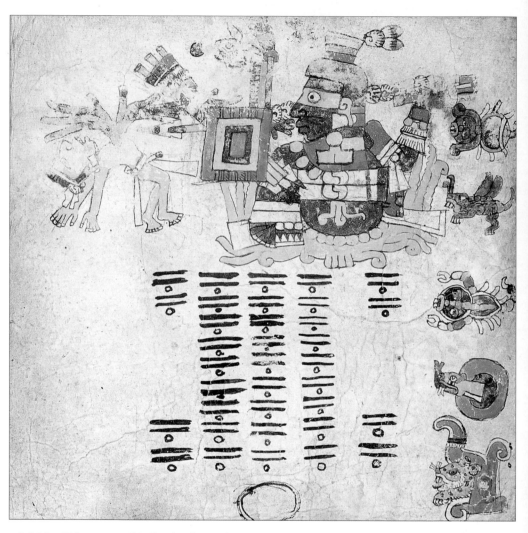

Above: The Aztec bar and dot counting system can be read in this page from the Codex Cospi *(c.1350–1500). Tezcatlipoca, lord of night and fate, is in warrior garb and equipped with weapons. The images to his right are symbols for calendrical dates.*

of 400s (20 units of 20), the line above that numbers of 8000s (20 units of 400) and so on. A single bar in the first line, with a dot in the line above, two bars in the line above and one bar in the line above would represent (1×5) plus (1×20) plus (10×400) plus (5×8000), which makes 5+20+4000+40,000=44,025.

The first breakthrough in deciphering the Maya bar and dot system was made in 1832 by Constantine Rafinesque (1783–1840), a brilliant naturalist and traveller-writer. Noticing the frequent use of bars and dots in the *Dresden Codex*, he surmised that these symbols were being used as numbers. He saw that the dots never appeared in groups of more than four and guessed that the bar stood for 5 and the dots for single units. Subsequently

Ernst Förstemann, archivist at Dresden where the codex was kept, discovered the Maya scribes' use of the shell symbol to stand for 0.

This system was used primarily to mark and record dates. However, the Maya apparently also used this positional mathematics for practical calculation. According to Diego de Landa, Maya merchants negotiating a deal would use grains of maize or cacao beans spread out on the dry ground or a flat rock to reckon

Above: The profiles of gods' heads carved on this Yaxchilán lintel stand for numbers. The inscribed date is 11 February AD526.

even large numbers. The writers of codices generally used the simple bar-and-dot system for writing dates, but the craftsmen who carved the Classic Period stelae sometimes produced a more elaborate version. Each number from 0 to 19 had its own patron divinity and stonemasons began to carve heads or full images of these gods to represent particular numbers. This practice was particularly common among the sculptors who produced the elegant stelae at Quiriguá and Copán. A well-known example is found on the east side of Stela D at Quiriguá, where the god of the number 7 (Uuk) is carved in place of the number. Another example, on a lintel at Yaxchilán, is illustrated above – gods' heads representing numbers are combined with animal carvings standing for cycles of time.

AZTEC NUMBERS

The Aztecs also used the bar and dot system. Some scholars believe the system to have been an ancient part of the shared

Right: Aztec numbers, from top left – 1, 2, 3, 4, 5, 6, 7, 8, 9, 10, 11, 12, 13, 14, 15, 16, 17, 18, 19, 20, 21, 22, 23, 24, 25, 29, 30, 40, 50, 55, 100, 101, 104, 114, 154, 600, 618, 1500 and 25,000.

Mesoamerican culture, possibly dating as far back back as the Olmec era (c.1500 –400BC). Like the Maya, the Aztecs seem to have been happy to use bars and dots to record dates in manuscripts and on monuments. However, because their growing empire drew in vast quantities of tribute from dependent territories, they also developed a system of number glyphs for use in accounting.

The newer system was still based on units of 20. A feather glyph meant 20, a flag glyph stood for 400 and a symbol representing a bag of incense was 8000 (20×400). A scribe who wanted to note receipt of 540 items of produce would draw one flag and seven feathers – 400 plus (7×20) = 540. He would generally draw a line alongside the glyphs to indicate they should be read in conjunction, then draw an image of the item received – say, a bag of cacao beans – and make a second line connecting the bag to the number. The readers of the tribute list would then understand that 540 bags of cacao beans had been received, counted and stored. Scholars would be able to decipher the system of number glyphs by

Above: The date carved on Lintel 26 at Yaxchilán marks the day on which King Shield Jaguar received his battle equipment from his wife: 9.14.12.6.12 in the Maya Long Count, or 12 February AD724.

examing the *Codex Mendoza* (c.1541). Part of this document comprises a detailed list of the tribute paid to Moctezuma II by subject towns and regions of the empire. It also has glosses in Spanish, written by an interpreter who understood the Nahuatl language and the Aztec system of numbers.

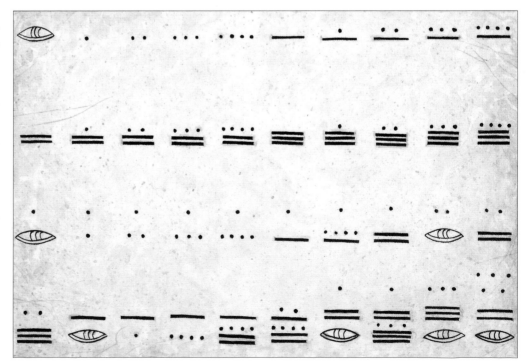

THREE INTO ONE: INTERLOCKING CALENDARS

The Aztec 365-day cycle contained 18 'months' of 20 days, plus five days at the year's end that were considered a time of ill omen. The 365-day count was called *xiuhpohualli* ('counting of the years') and was used for plotting religious festivals and for marking the seasons. The Aztec 260-day calendar combined the numbers 1–13 with 20 names of creatures, objects or forces such as crocodile, house, wind, flint knife, jaguar and reed. When the calendar was written down, each day name was denoted by a hieroglyph showing the object, animal or force, while each number was shown by dots. The cycle was called *tonalpohualli* ('the counting of the

days'). It began with 1-Crocodile, 2-Wind and 3-House. The thirteenth and fourteenth names in the cycle were reed and jaguar, but there was no fourteen in the number sequence, so after 13-Reed the *tonalpohualli* proceeded to 1-Jaguar,

Above: This Aztec carving represents a 52-year cycle or 'bundle of years'. A bundle of sticks was burned to celebrate a new cycle.

and then carried on through the day names while prefixing the numbers 2, 3, 4 and so on. The cycle was therefore divided into 20 'weeks' of 13 days, which the Spanish called *trecena*.

Together, the *tonalpohualli* or day count and the *xiuhpohualli* or year count produced 18,980 unique combinations before repeating the same intersection of days in the two calendars. This was the equivalent of 73 years in the *tonalpohualli* calendar or 52 years – the 'bundle of years' – in the *xiuhpohualli* calendar.

RELIGIOUS FESTIVALS

In the year calendar, each 20-day month was associated with a religious festival. Most were linked to the agricultural year and there were three principal kinds. One group honoured the sun, the land and maize. A second included offerings to mountains and sources of water, while a third paid homage to patron deities.

Some of the days of the calendar marked religious festivals, but priestly ceremonies were usually timed according to the year calendar. Priestly astronomers also looked to the heavens, in particular to the movements of the moon and Venus, when attempting to divine the events of the future.

Below: A Codex Borbonicus *image shows the deities Ometecuhtli and Omecihuatl creating the divinely ordained calendar.*

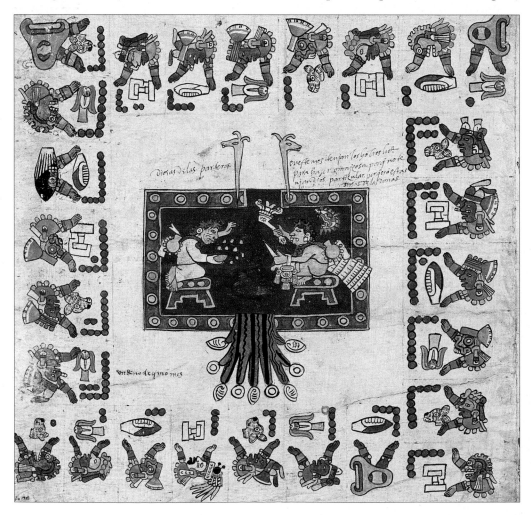

The five-day period at year's end, the *nemontemi*, was a time of withdrawal. People did not carry out their normal activities. Fields were left untended and markets were deserted. Householders broke their plates and utensils, fasted and let their fires go out. They even refrained from talking. One ritual looked to the new beginning the Aztecs hoped would follow the New Fire rites: a pregnant woman was locked in a granary in the hope that her fertility would be transferred to the corn.

The patterns of intersection between the two calendars meant that a new year in the *xiuhpohualli* could only begin on one of four possible names from the *tonalpohualli*. These were rabbit, reed, flint knife and house. Each year took its

Above: On the Aztec Sun Stone, the glyphs in the enclosed circle surrounding the sun god are those of the 20 days of the week.

name from the 'year bearer', whichever one of these four day-names fell on the first day of the new year. Within a 52-year cycle, the year bearers were numbered one to 13 in succession – 1-Rabbit, 2-Reed, 3-House, 4-Flint-knife, 5-Rabbit, 6-Reed, 7-House, 8-Flint-knife, 9-Rabbit, 10-Reed, 11-House, 12-Flint-knife, 13-Rabbit, 1-Reed, 2-House and so on.

Because there were 20 days in each month of the *xiuhpohualli* and a recurring pattern of 20 day-signs in the *tonalpohualli*, each month in the *tonalpohualli* began with the same day-sign as the year. That is, the year-bearer was also the 'month-bearer'. The year-bearer was also celebrated repeatedly throughout the year.

Among the Aztecs, the 52-year cycles were not differentiated from each other. The date system could specify that an event took place on a particular day in a particular year within a 52-year cycle, but not in which 52-year cycle it happened. This presented significant

problems in long cycles of time. The problem was solved by the 'Long Count', which marked time from a year zero in the distant past. Scholars believe the Long Count was widely used in Mesoamerica in early times, but that it fell into disuse in all except Maya lands, where it was developed into a sophisticated system.

THE MAYA CALENDAR

The Maya used the same combination of a 260-day ritual count with 13 20-day cycles and a 365-day solar count with 18 20-day months and a five-day unlucky period at year's end. The Maya called the 260-day calendar the *tzolkin*, and the 365-day calendar the *haab*. Scholars sometimes call the 365-day measure the 'Vague Year' because Mesoamericans did not take account of the fact that a solar year lasts slightly more than 365 days and add an extra day every four years. Nor did they make any of the other sophisticated adjustments of the Gregorian calendar now widely used in the West. Over time, their solar year must have dragged behind the movements of the stars and sun.

Bishop Diego de Landa gave a detailed description of the Maya calendars and made careful note of the glyphs used by the Maya for day-signs and months. To give a day its full Maya calendrical date would require the *tzolkin* date and the *haab* date. For example, 13 Ahau 18 Cumku. This date would have been towards the close of the final month before the unlucky five-day period (*uayeb*) at the end of the year.

Below: The 20 Aztec day names are (from top left) flower, rain, flint knife, movement, vulture, eagle, jaguar, reed, grass, monkey, dog, water, rabbit, deer, death, serpent, lizard, house, wind and crocodile.

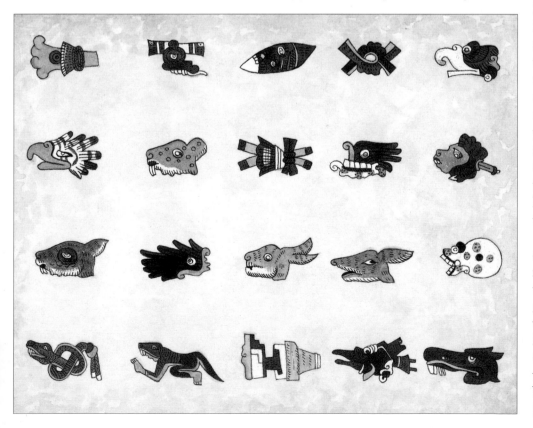

COUNTING THE DAYS

Scholars cannot agree why the early Mesoamericans first fixed on 260 days as a useful unit for measuring time. Some have argued that it was based on observation of the movements of Venus and of the sun in our skies. The 260-day period roughly corresponds to the gap between the appearance of Venus as the evening star and its emergence as the morning star. There is also an interval of 260 days between the sun's annual southward movement and its northward return when viewed from a latitude close to Copán. This celestial observation might have been used to time planting and harvest and over centuries it could have become a hallowed measurement strongly associated with divine rhythms underlying fertility.

HUMAN RHYTHMS

Most modern scholars argue that the 260-day cycle is based on human rhythms. Midwives may have used the measure, counting forward 260 days

Above: At El Tajin, Mexico, the Pyramid of the Niches has 365 niches, supposedly one for each day of the solar year.

from the date of a woman's last menstrual period, to predict when a baby would be likely to be born, as do the modern Maya still living in the mountains of southern Guatemala. The 260-day calendar has proved a most enduring invention. It is still used among the Quiché inhabitants of the tropical mountains of southern Guatemala.

THE MAYA LONG COUNT

In addition to the twinned 260-day and 365-day calendars, the Maya people greatly refined a much longer-running measuring system, the 'Long Count', which is known to have been used in many parts of Mesoamerica at the start of the first millennium BC. During the Classic Period (c. AD250–900), the Maya dated their monuments using the Long Count to record births, deaths, royal accessions and anniversaries, the dates of ritual sacrifices and battle

Left: The 20 Maya day names include Imix (top left), Akbal (centre top), Etznab (centre bottom) and Ahau (bottom right).

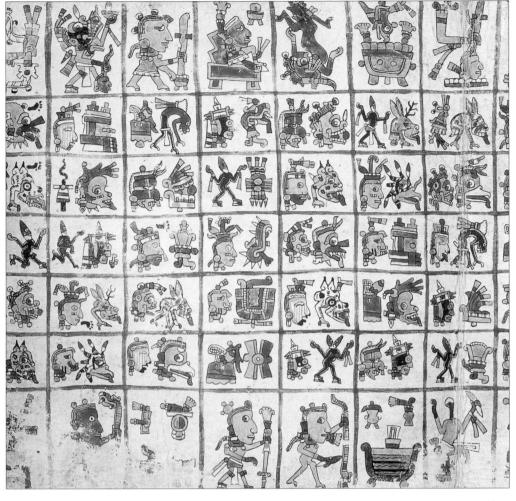

triumphs. This system counted forward from a zero date of 4 Ahua 8 Cumku, equivalent to 11 August 3114BC in the Gregorian calendar.

The Maya Long Count counted days in units of 20 and used a 'year' of 360 days. Its five units were the *baktun* (144,000 days), the *katun* (7,200 days), the *tun* (360 days), the *uinal* (20 days) and the *kin* (1 day). Dates were carved in this order, with units separated by full points. For example, the date 3.3.2.1.1 would be three *baktuns* (432,000 days), three *katuns* (21,600 days), 2 *tuns* (720 days), one *uinal* (20 days) and 1 *kin* (1 day), making a total of 454,341 days after the zero date of 11 August 3114BC.

The earliest Maya Long Count inscription is from El Baúl on the Pacific coast in the southern Maya or highland Maya region and dates to AD37.

A date carved on a stela gave the Long Count followed by the position in the Calendar Round (the combination of

Above: The Mixtec Codex Cospi (c.1350–1500) contains a ritual calendar and a detailed survey of the movements of Venus.

the *haab* calendar and the *tzolkin* calendar). Because there are so very many dates on stelae, early scholars thought that the Maya worshipped time itself. However, breakthroughs in understanding hieroglyphics enabled the successors of those scholars to grasp that the dates were provided to set in time the image carved beneath them of a king's accession or triumph over a rival ruler.

The Long Count date is usually only carved once on a stela: dates given later for the ruler's birth-date or accession are almost invariably given only in the *tzolkin* calendar because the larger context of the Long Count date has already been established. Dates on stelae also often provide information about the moon. Scholars call the Long Count and Calendar Round dates, which come first in inscriptions, the 'Initial Series' and the information on the moon cycle the 'Lunar Series'.

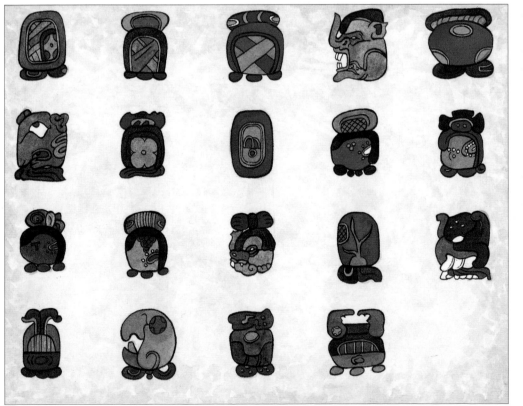

Left: The glyphs for the 19 Maya months include Pop (top left), Zotz (top, fourth from left), Pax (bottom left) and Uayeb (last).

MAJOR AZTEC FESTIVALS

AZTEC MONTH 1
Western dates 14 February–5 March
Festival name Atlcaualo (The Ending of Water), Cuauhitleua (The Lifting of Trees)
Gods/goddesses honoured Tláloc (rain and fertility god), Chalchiúhtlicue (goddess of springs, rivers and the sea), Chicomecóatl (maize goddess), Xilonen (maize goddess), Quetzalcóatl (storms, wind and rain god)
Rites Offerings to maize divinities, including the sacrifice of children; banners erected in homes and temples.

AZTEC MONTH 2
Western dates 6–25 March
Festival name Tlacaxipehualiztli (Skinning of the Men)
Gods/goddesses honoured Xipe Totec (god of vegetation and spring, patron of goldworkers)
Rites Victims slaughtered, priests wear their skin over their face and body; five prisoners of war killed in staged combat; *tlatoani* takes part in dance and military ritual.

AZTEC MONTH 3
Western dates 26 March–14 April
Festival name Tozoztontli (Minor Vigil), Xochimanaloya (Presentation of flowers)
Gods/goddesses honoured Tláloc (rain and fertility god), Chalchiúhtlicue (goddess of springs, rivers and the sea), Centéotl (maize god), Coatlícue (earth goddess)
Rites Ceremonial planting of seeds; donations of flowers to the festival deities; priests made offering of flayed skins.

AZTEC MONTH 4
Western dates 15 April–4 May (End of dry season)
Festival name Huey Tozoztli (Major Vigil)
Gods/goddesses honoured Tláloc (rain and fertility god), Chalchiúhtlicue (goddess of springs, rivers and the sea), Centéotl (maize god), Coatlícue (earth goddess), Chicomecóatl (maize goddess), Xilonen (maize goddess), Quetzalcóatl (storms, wind and rain god)
Rites Rulers of Tenochtitlán, Texcoco, Tlacopán and Xochimilco made sacrifices to the earth; a girl impersonating Chalchiúhtlicue was sacrificed and her blood poured on Lake Texcoco; priestesses of Chicomecóatl bless farmers' seed supplies.

AZTEC MONTH 5
Western dates 5–22 May
Festival name Tóxcatl (Drought)
Gods/goddesses honoured Tezcatlipoca (god of fate, kingship and other attributes), Huitzilopochtli (México tribal god, also god of war and associated with the sun), Mixcóatl (hunt god), Camaxtli (hunt god)
Rites Youth who has impersonated Tezcatlipoca for a year sacrificed on the Great Pyramid in Tenochtitlán; impersonators of Huitzilopochtli, Mixcóatl and Camaxtli sacrificed separately.

AZTEC MONTH 6
Western dates 23 May–13 June (Start of rainy season)
Festival name Etzalcualiztli (Meal of Maize and Beans)
Gods/goddesses honoured Tláloc (rain and fertility god), Chalchiúhtlicue (goddess of waters), Quetzalcóatl (wind and rain god)
Rites Priests held vigils and fasts, praying for a cloudburst; noblemen danced with maize stalks; new reeds harvested on the lake; meals of maize and beans served.

AZTEC MONTH 7
Western dates 14 June–3 July
Festival name Tecuilhuitontli (Minor Festival of the Lords)
Gods/goddesses honoured Xochipilli (god of flowers, song and dance), Huixtocíhuatl (goddess of salt)
Rites *Tlatoani* dance in public and hand out gifts to the people; nobility hold feasts open to commoners; sacrifices made to salt goddess and to Xochipilli.

AZTEC MONTH 8
Western dates 4–23 July
Festival name Huey Tecuilhuitl (Major Festival of the Lords)
Gods/goddesses honoured Xilonen (maize goddess), Cihuacóatl (fertility goddess)
Rites *Tlatoani* dance and hand out gifts; nobility hold feasts for commoners to celebrate the appearance of the first maize shoots; offerings made to a girl who is impersonating Xilonen.

AZTEC MONTH 9
Western dates 24 July–12 August
Festival name Miccailhuitontli (Minor Festival of the Dead), Tlaxochimaco (Emergence of Flowers)
Gods/goddesses honoured Tezcatlipoca (god of fate, kingship, darkness, masculinity and many other attributes), Huitzilopochtli (México tribal god, also god of war and associated with the sun), ancestor gods
Rites Sacrifices to Huitzilopochtli in his guise as the ancestral leader of the migrating México; offerings made to the dead; feasts and dances held in their honour.

AZTEC MONTH 10

Western dates 13 August–
1 September
Festival name Huey Miccailhuitl
(Major Festival of the Dead),
Xocotlhuetzi (Ripening of the
Xocotl fruit)
Gods/goddesses honoured
Huehuetéotl (old fire god), Xiuhtecuhtli
(fire god), Yacatecuhtli (trader's god)
Rites Fire sacrifices; offerings made
to ancestors.

AZTEC MONTH 11

Western dates 2–21 September (Start
of harvest)
Festival name Ochpaniztli (Clearing)
Gods/goddesses honoured Toci
(earth goddess), Tlazoltéotl (goddess
of love and filth), Teteoinnan (earth
goddess), Coatlícue (earth goddess),
Cinteotl (maize goddess), Chicomecóatl
(maize goddess)
Rites Female sacrificial victim
beheaded and flayed by priestess
of Xilonen-Chicomecóatl, who then
wore her skin; corn seeds thrown to
the people; cleaning and repairs
carried out. Preparations for the
approaching season of war included
military manoeuvres; *tlatoani* gives
insignia to soldiers. Priests started a
major fast that ran until the Festival
of Panquetzalitzli.

AZTEC MONTH 12

Western dates 22 September–11 October
(Harvest)
Festival name Teotleco (Coming of the
Gods and Goddesses)
Gods/goddesses honoured All
Rites General festivities included
dancing and feasting; footprint
made at midnight in a bowl of
maize flour in the temple signified
the coming of the gods and
the goddesses.

AZTEC MONTH 13

Western dates 12–31 October
Festival name Tepeilhuitl (Festival of
the Mountains)
Gods/goddesses honoured Tláloc
(rain god), *Tlaloque* (rain god's
assistants), Tepictoton (rain god), Octli
(deities of *pulque* drink), Xochiquetzal
(flower goddess) and divine mountains
Popocatépetl, Ixtaccíhuatl (Mount)
Tlaloc and Matlalcueye
Rites Ritual offerings made at
mountain sanctuaries.

AZTEC MONTH 14

Western dates 1–20 November
Festival name Quecholli (Treasured
Feather)
Gods/goddesses honoured Mixcóatl
(hunt god), Camaxtli (hunt god)
Rites Hunting competitions held;
prisoners dressed as deer sacrificed
in honour of the hunt gods; soldiers
fast in preparation for war; weapons
made for battle and hunting.

AZTEC MONTH 15

Western dates 21 November–
10 December
Festival name Panquetzalitzi (Lifting
of the Banners)
Gods/goddesses honoured Tezcatlipoca
(god of fate, kingship, darkness,
masculinity and many other attributes),
Huitzilopochtli (México tribal god, also
god of war and associated with the sun)
Rites Major sacrifices of prisoners of war,
including sacrifice of the 'bathed slaves';
sacred procession from the Great
Pyramid to Tlatelolco, Chapultepec and
Coyoacan, then back to the sacred
precinct at Tenochtitlán; paper banners
hung on houses and in fruit trees.

AZTEC MONTH 16

Western dates 11–30 December
Festival name Atemoztli (Coming
Down of Waters)
Gods/goddesses honoured Tláloque
(rain god's assistants) and divine
mountains Popocatépetl, Ixtaccihuatl
(Mount) Tláloc and Matlalcueye
Rites Ceremonies held in honour of
the mountains.

AZTEC MONTH 17

Western dates 31 December–
19 January
Festival name Tititl (Stretching)
Gods/goddesses honoured Cihuacóatl
(fertility goddess), Ilamatecuhtli
(ancient mother goddess), Tonantzin
(mother goddess), Yacatecuhtli (god
of traders and travellers)
Rites Merchants offer slave sacrifices to
Yacatecuhtli; weavers made offerings
to Ilamatecuhtli; public dancing involving
priests, nobility and the *tlatoani*.

AZTEC MONTH 18

Western dates 20 January–8 February
Festival name Izcalli (Growing)
Gods/goddesses honoured
Xiuhtecuhtli (fire god), Tláloc
(rain god), Chalchiúhtlicue
(water goddess)
Rites Animal sacrifices to the fire
god; corn toasted and tamales
served with greens; dough effigies
of Xiuhtecuhtli made.

The five days at the end of the year
(9–13 February) were a time for doing
as little as possible to avoid ill fortune.
People stayed at home and did not do
any business.

DIVINING THE FUTURE

Priests used the ritual calendar to divine the future. Aztec priests consulted long screenfold books called *tonalamatl*. In these books, which were made from bark paper coated with a white mineral paste, scribes recorded the calendar and the many meanings of its cycles.

ARCANE MEANINGS

The calendars contained a rich blend of arcane meanings. Each number in the *tonalpohualli* was under a divine influence. Each of the 13 lords of the day was associated with a butterfly or bird. Each of the day-names also had its associated deity (see chart). A further cycle of nine lords of the night cast its influence over the calendar. The influences that were in place at the start of each 13-day period remained a powerful force throughout.

Below: A priest on this pre-Toltec stela from Santa Lucia Cotzumalhuapa uses a staff to help make an astronomical observation.

AZTEC DAY GODS IN THE *TONALPOHUALLI*		
Day	**Symbol**	**God**
1	Crocodile (cipactli)	Tonacatecuhtli (Creator god)
2	Wind (éhecatl)	Quetzalcóatl (Storm/wind god among many other attributes)
3	House (calli)	Tepeyolohtli (God of regeneration)
4	Lizard (cuetzpallin)	Huehuecóyotl (Old Old Coyote, a trickster god)
5	Serpent (cóatl)	Chalchiúhtlicue (Water goddess)
6	Death (miquiztli)	Tecciztécatl (Moon god)
7	Deer (mázatl)	Tláloc (Rain god)
8	Rabbit (tochtli)	Mayáhuel (Maguey plant goddess)
9	Water (atl)	Xiuhtecuhtli (Fire god)
10	Dog (izcuintli)	Mictlantecuhtli (Lord of the underworld)
11	Monkey (ozomatli)	Xochipilli (God of flowers, song and dance)
12	Grass (malinalli)	Patécatl (Medicine god)
13	Reed (ácatl)	Tezcatlipoca (God of night and destiny, among many other attributes)
14	Jaguar (océlotl)	Tlazoltéotl (Goddess of filth and love)
15	Eagle (cuauhtli)	Xipe Totec (Vegetation god)
16	Vulture (cozcacuauhtli)	Itzapapálotl (A form of Coatlícue, an earth goddess)
17	Motion (ollin)	Xólotl (double of Quetzalcóatl)
18	Flint (técpatl)	Tezcatlipoca
19	Rain (quiáhuitl)	Chantico (Hearth goddess)
20	Flower (xóchitl)	Xochiquetzal (Flower goddess)

The Maya understood that the last day of each solar month fell under the influence of the month that was about to begin. The 20th day of Zotz, for example, was influenced by the next month, Tzec, and was said to be 'the seating of Tzec'. The following day was 1-Tzec. A baby's destiny might be read in the influences prevalent on its birthday. Parents whose child was born on an ill-omened day could improve his or her chances by holding a naming ceremony on a day that carried positive associations.

Priests consulted the movements of celestial bodies. Priest-astrologer-diviners would plot the best days for planting, harvesting and other daily activities. For example, Maya planting books instructed farmers on which days to plant during the months of Chen and Yax.

Below: Priests determined the auspicious date for ceremonies. This marker from the Maya city of Chinkultic says that the ball court was dedicated on 21 May AD591.

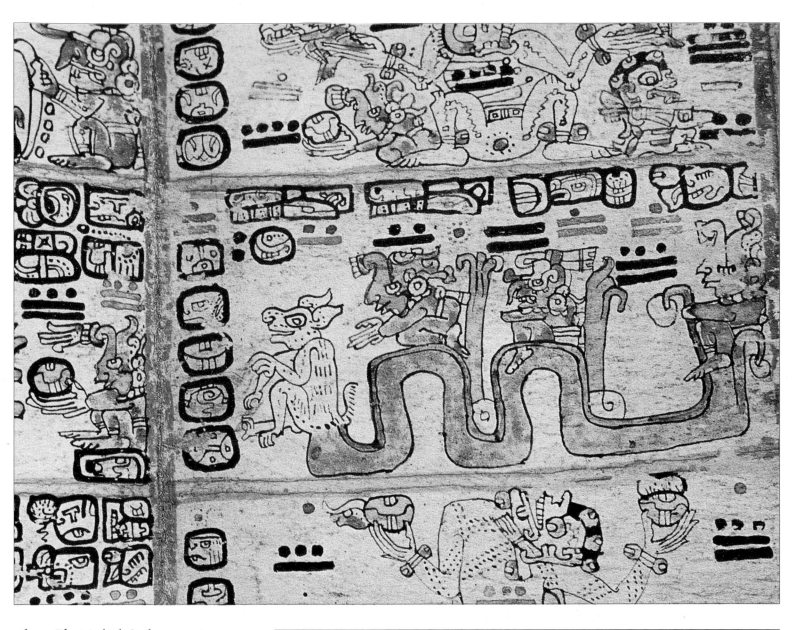

Above: The Madrid Codex *contains almanacs used by priests for timing religious rites and plotting astronomical movements.*

Merchants would take diviners' advice when planning their departure and return dates for journeys. In the Maya realms, rulers would visit the astronomer-priests to check on celestial movements: they often launched attacks to coincide with the rising of the malign planet Venus. Fittingly, the Maya hieroglyph for war consists of the logograph for Venus (one image representing the whole word) combined with another sign.

Among the Aztecs, the *tlatoani* himself and his advisers would take account of the meanings of the calendars and the heavens when plotting military campaigns. Indeed, it was one of the *tlatoani*'s duties to scan the heavens for guidance.

DAYKEEPERS AND MODERN DIVINING

Anthropologists have discovered modern diviners at work using the 260-day calendar in Guatemala.

Shaman-priests who are known as 'daykeepers' work among the Quiché people of Momostenango in Guatemala, using the ritual calendar to divine solutions for people's problems. Burning copal incense, they take a handful of coral seeds and count them out in piles of four. The number left over at the end provides information about the problem. The priest then counts the number of piles and counts back the same number of days through the 260-day round to give an indication of when the problem began. He or she may feel a 'lightning' in the blood when counting past a particular day, which gives further information to be interpreted. At this moment, the priest's body becomes an image of the universe in microcosm. The sensations he or she feels have meaning in a larger context. The priest makes use of the many associations of each day-sign to intuit the arrangements of cosmic energy around the individual and his or her difficulty, and so work out a possible response to the problem.

The Momostenango Quiché have safeguarded many traditional Maya religious practices. They hold a celebrated religious festival in which new daykeepers are initiated on the day 8-Monkey in the 260-day calendar.

READING THE STARS

In Mesoamerican societies, priests were guardians of time. As well as computing the calendar and keeping track of festivals and necessary religious ceremonies, they watched the movements of the stars and planets for bad omens or propitious dates. By interpreting the movements of the celestial bodies, priests could gain knowledge of the divinely inspired future. Among the Maya, the priest was known as Ah Kin ('Servant of the Sun'), making clear his connection to both astronomy and the calendar. As timekeeper, the Maya priest-scribe was also in charge of the genealogies of the city-state.

UNIVERSAL FORCES

Just as the priests understood the pattern of days and weeks in the ritual and solar calendars to be full of divine energy and meaning, so they saw the orbits and phases of the planets and the movements of stars to be a manifestation of

Below: The circular Venus observatory in Chichén Itzá was built to let astronomers observe the four phases of the planet Venus.

universal forces that impacted upon the lives of men. The movements of the planet Venus were considered of great importance. In Mesoamerican latitudes, Venus shines brilliantly in the morning sky, as large as a tennis ball. The planet assumed an important role in religion and mythology.

Venus follows a near-circular orbit around the sun: one orbit takes 225 days. Like the moon, Venus goes through a number of phases: one cycle of phases takes 584 days. The Mesoamerican astronomers knew about this because they had measured it from observatory-towers such as the ones in the Maya cities of Mayapán and Chichén Itzá. They knew that Venus goes through four phases. It rises first in the morning sky

Left: The standing figure on this terracotta incense burner from Palenque may be the Maya sun god.

and is visible as the morning star for 236 days. Thereafter it disappears into the light of the sun and is lost to sight for 90 days. At the end of this period it rises in the evening sky and is visible as the evening star for 250 days. In its fourth phase, it is invisible for eight days before reappearing as the morning star.

PHASES OF VENUS

The Maya associated the 'invisible phases' of Venus, when the planet disappears from view, with voyages to the spirit realm of the underworld. Quetzalcóatl's descent to the underworld to claim the bones of fishmen, the 'people' of a previous world-age, was understood to take place during the eight-day phase when Venus is invisible. When Quetzalcóatl returned successfully from his task, he rose into the heavens as the morning star. Every Maya ruler was thought to travel to the underworld after death and, if he passed successfully through the trials he encountered there, would rise into the skies as Venus.

In another tradition Quetzalcóatl-Topiltzin, overcome with shame after being outwitted by his dark double Tezcatlipoca and brought to sleep with his sister, takes his own life on a blazing pyre. From the flames his heart rises as Venus the morning star.

The appearance of Venus as the morning star would appear to be a reminder of the king's immortality and a celebration of the victory of Quetzalcóatl over the lords of the spirit realm and over death. Yet Venus did not generally have positive

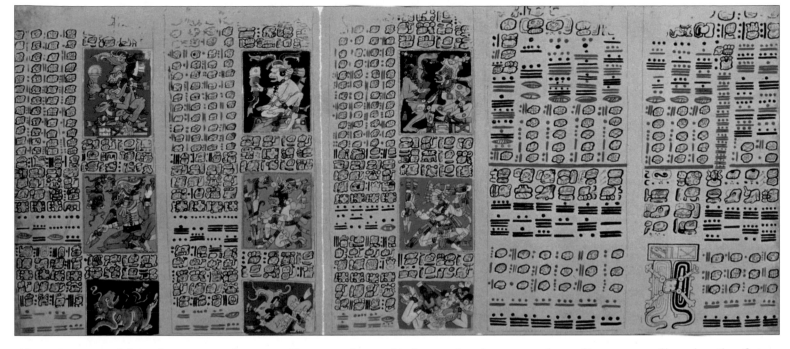

Above: Priests used the information in these pages from the Dresden Codex *to calculate the future cycles of the planet Venus.*

associations in the Mesoamerican mind. The planet was believed to have a negative influence on earthly affairs.

MAYA OBSERVATORIES

Maya star-watchers, who had no specialized astronomical equipment, predicted the rising of Venus as morning star and evening star with astonishing accuracy; to within one day in 6,000 years. The tower-observatory in the Maya city of Chichén Itzá tells of the dedication with which Maya priests plotted celestial movements. The tower is known in modern times as the Caracol, from the Spanish for snail, because it has spiral passageways. It was built for observation of Venus. Three passages leaving the Caracol line up precisely with the spots in the western sky where Venus can be seen as the evening star, among them the most northerly and southerly point at which it sets. At Palenque, the square tower that rises above the palace is decorated with a Venus glyph and appears to have been used as an observatory for plotting the planet's movements, while at Uxmal, the Governor's Palace must have been used for astronomical observation. It is aligned with a mound above which Venus would have risen at the most southerly point in its cycle.

Priests also relied on books to plot celestial movements. The *Grolier Codex* of *c.*1230 consists of around half of a table for predicting the Venus cycle over 104 years. The *Dresden Codex*, which dates to just before the Spanish Conquest, contains tables for plotting the Venus and Mars cycles and solar eclipses, as well as details of rites and deities associated with the 260-day calendar. Both these books contain eight-year Venus tables which show that the Maya understood how, after five 584-day Venus cycles and eight 365-day solar cycles, the two met ($5\times584 = 2920$ days $= 8\times365$).

GODS AND ANIMALS: THE MAYA ZODIAC

There is disagreement among scholars over whether the Maya had a zodiac of star-signs like that developed by Western astrologers.

Some authors believe that there is evidence for a Maya zodiac on a badly damaged page of the *Paris Codex*, which shows animals hanging from a band thought to represent the heavens. The *Paris Codex* animals are a scorpion, a turtle and a rattlesnake. We know that the Maya saw a constellation in the night sky by the name of *tzab* ('rattlesnake rattle') where in the western tradition we see the Pleiades.

It is likely that a Maya zodiac would contain the turtle, because that creature plays an important role in Maya creation stories. In some accounts, the world was said to be lying atop a giant turtle; there is also an image on a surviving Maya pot of the maize god rising from the broken earth, which is represented by a broken turtle shell.

Scholars believe that the Maya may have associated the stars of our constellation Orion with a turtle. In one of the murals at Bonampak a turtle is shown with the three stars from Orion's belt adorning its shell.

Among the Aztecs, most of the gods had equivalents among the stars. Tezcatlipoca was associated with the Great Bear. The jaguar skin that he was often shown wearing was an Aztec image for the night sky itself. Aztecs believed that the Great Bear's descent into the waters of the ocean was a re-enactment of the myth in which Tezcatlipoca loses his foot while he is fighting the Earth Monster. Quetzalcóatl was Venus as the morning star and the same planet as the evening star was Quetzalcóatl's double, Xólotl, who travelled with the Plumed Serpent to the underworld when he went to outwit the underworld lords and launch the current world-age.

WRITTEN RECORDS

The Olmec peoples who flourished on the Gulf Coast of Mexico c.1500–400 BC are accorded the honour of being the first Mesoamerican people to develop a written script by some scholars. On one end of a basalt column from the Olmec site at La Venta, a craftsman carved the relief of a walking man with a beard and beside the man's head cut three signs that

Below: A scribe incised Maya glyphs into this jade pendant in the 5th century AD. Added red colour makes reading easier.

look like hieroglyphs. Experts have been unable to decipher the signs, but suggest that one of the glyph-like images, which looks like a bird's head, probably represents the man's name.

Other examples of Olmec hieroglyph-like images are found on pots and celts of jade and serpentine. But most scholars now argue that while the Olmec certainly used symbols to communicate meaning, their carvings cannot be called writing because the symbols do not refer to the sounds of a language. They are symbols purely and simply. Like road signs, they carry meaning, but do not represent sounds or words.

FIRST BOOKS

Intriguingly, it appears that the Olmec might already have been using screenfold books made from *amate* bark. A ceramic bowl that might be dated as early as 1200 BC is carved with two objects that resemble this kind of book. The Olmec appear to have had a working system of written communication even if it was not writing as we define it.

Following the collapse of Olmec culture, the Zapotec craftsmen of Monte Albán in c.600–200 BC were the next to develop the art of writing in Mesoamerica. They carved images of male figures in the Temple of the Danzantes at Monte Albán alongside hieroglyphic signs that appear to represent the figures' names.

The men depicted were once thought to be dancers (*danzantes*) but are now believed to be sacrificed war captives. Later Zapotec monuments bear longer texts that include dates in the Calendar Round, cut with year signs, glyphs for days and months and bar-and-dot numbers. As with the Olmec inscriptions, scholars have been unable to decipher these carvings, apart from the dates. The earliest example of Zapotec writing is probably the stone called Monument 3 from San José Mogote in the Oaxaca Valley. It depicts a slain captive with

Above: The top section of this carving shows Aztec rulers Tizoc and Ahuítzotl. Beneath are the glyphs representing the date 8-Reed.

blood pouring from his chest and gives the Calendar date 1-Earthquake – perhaps his day-name. It has been dated to c.600 BC.

Some scholars claim this as the earliest example of Mesoamerican writing and argue that other forms derived from the Zapotec, but other authorities suggest that this was just one of several scripts that the inventive Mesoamericans developed independently in the years after the decline of the Olmec. Two monuments carved with Long Count dates survive from c.30 BC, one in Chiapas and one in Veracruz. Neither has an accompanying hieroglyphic text, so it is impossible to judge the development of writing locally at that stage.

THE ISTHMIAN SCRIPT

A writing system known as the 'Isthmian script' appears to have been used in southern Veracruz in the 2nd century AD.

Only four objects carved with this script survive. The most important are a jade figure known as the Tuxtla statuette, now in the Smithsonian Institution, Washington, DC, and a basalt stela found in 1986 at La Mojarra in Veracruz. The script used only 150 signs, so scholars argue these signs probably represented whole words rather than phonetic elements (the distinctive sounds of a language). Some of the signs used bear superficial resemblance to later Maya signs, but experts believe the Isthmian script was not a close relative of early Maya writing. Maya writing was read in double columns from left to right and also top to bottom. However, the Isthmian script does not link its columns in twos and may not have been read left to right, for the glyphs appear to face towards a standing figure in the centre of the carving.

Below: This stone calendar, inscribed with glyphs, was carved by a craftsman of the Huastec culture in north-eastern Mexico.

Carving found on a stone stela at Kaminaljuyú (near modern Guatemala City) from around the same time appears to have a much greater similarity to Maya scripts. The inscription does use paired columns as in Maya writing, and it may contain some of the same glyphs. Indeed, the carving may even be in Maya writing, but is too fragmentary to provide definitive evidence.

The earliest surviving piece definitely identified in the Maya writing system is the Hauberg stela of AD199. The stela shows a king wearing the mask of the rain god Chac and the two-headed

Above: In the intriguing Zapotec carvings that depict war sacrifices at Monte Albán, a number of early glyphs are believed to give the victims' names.

serpent that indicates royal standing. The dating inscription does not include a Long Count date, but the scholar Linda Schele has interpreted the given date to be AD199. The inscription uses the emblem glyph, which is commonly found in Maya inscriptions. The emblem glyph generally identifies the ruler as *k'ul ahaw* ('holy king') of a particular city, in this case, puzzlingly, the 'holy king of Fire'.

ROYAL SCRIBES AND CODICES

Scribes were members of the Maya elite. They were usually the sons and daughters of nobles or even royalty. A late Classic Period vase thought to have been made at Naranjo was signed by the artist Ah Maxam, who wrote that he was the son of a king of Naranjo and a princess from Yaxhá. Many kings appear to have been scribes. They are shown on vases wearing a bundle of pens in their hair, which was an accepted mark of high-ranking scribal office. Royal sons and daughters were doubtless educated in scribal schools.

The most important scribe in the Classic Period Maya city state was the *ak k'u hun* ('guardian of the sacred books').

Below: A skilled Maya stonecutter incised 32 hieroglyphs on this lintel at Yaxchilán. The work is dated AD534.

THE DUTIES OF SCRIBES

From the evidence of images on Maya vases in murals, the chief scribe or *ak k'u hun* had many courtly jobs in addition to artistic endeavours. He or she was expected to arrange royal ceremonies, was a negotiator of royal marriages and a record-keeper responsible for recording offerings of tribute from client states or allies and keeping royal genealogical lists. He or she may also have taught in scribal schools.

The Maya scribe probably painted the images that accompanied his words. Both calligraphers and painters were given the title *ah ts'ib* ('he of the writing'). Those who produced hieroglyphic inscriptions and images in stone were accorded the honour of being named *yuxul* ('sculptor'). Both women and men – although probably more men than women – were scribes. The titles *ah ts'ib* and *ak k'u hun* were given to women and men.

Above: Maya scribes also cut glyphs in wood, but little of their work has survived. This is a lintel from Temple IV at Tikal.

Students at scribe schools must have followed long and demanding courses of study, for reading and writing Maya hieroglyphs required great knowledge and skill. A scribe had many choices when writing. He or she could write the same phrase in a number of ways. Some logographs (images representing whole words) could also be used as phonetic signs (symbols representing spoken sounds). Scribes sometimes used both the logograph for a name or word and the phonetic signs that would spell out that name. An example often given by Maya experts is that the word *balam* ('jaguar'), could be written with a single logograph representing the head of a jaguar, with the logograph and

GODS OF THE SCRIBES

One 8th-century AD Maya vase depicts a rabbit deity writing in a screenfold book. The creature is one of the large number of gods who are associated with Maya scribes.

Itzamná, the supreme Maya god, was believed to be the creator of writing, and is shown as a scribe in the *Madrid Codex*. Itzamná's animal form was a bearded dragon: carvings at Copán show scribes emerging from the mouth of this creature. Another high-ranking Maya god, Pawahtún, was often shown in images of scribes and on one vase is seen teaching novice scribes in an elite school. The Monkey-men, half-brothers of the Hero Twins in the *Popol Vuh* cycle, are often portrayed with writing implements or working at codices. Both the Hero Twins' father, the Young Maize God, and Hunahpú, one of the Twins, were associated with kingship and writing. They, too, were often shown with quill pens working at calligraphy. The rabbit deity was linked to the moon goddess. Mesoamericans thought they saw a rabbit in the face of the moon whereas in Western tradition we think we see a man's figure or a man's face.

some phonetic signs, and also with the three phonetic signs that spelled *ba*, *la* and *ma*.

Some signs were both logographs and phonetic signs. To help readers know in which way a sign was being used, scribes often used additional phonetic signs alongside the logographs.

On most Classic Period Maya monuments, the hieroglyphs are written to be read in paired columns from left to right and also from top to bottom: you read the first line/first column, first line/second column, then second line/first

Right: A terracotta figure left as an offering on Jaina Island represents a noble or perhaps princely scribe at work.

column, second line/second column etc. Some shorter pieces of writing on monuments and on ceramic objects and carved bones or shells were arranged differently; sometimes as horizontal lines, sometimes as vertical lines. An intriguing variation, found on the markers of ball courts and on some altars, was for the text to be arranged in a circle; the reader would know by a marker in the text (usually a date) where to begin reading. At Quiriguá and Copán, hieroglyphs are sometimes written on monuments in a complex criss-cross pattern to resemble a woven mat. In a very few cases – for example, Lintel 25 at Yaxchilán and on four pages of the *Paris Codex* – the hieroglyphs were inscribed to be read from right to left.

MAYA WRITING

Surviving Maya writing is of various kinds. The stelae of Classic Period Maya cities such as Yaxchilán, Tikal and Copán celebrate the achievements of holy kings and the dynasties to which they belonged. However, the northern Maya cities such as Uxmal and Chichén Itzá that continued to thrive after the 'Maya Collapse' in the lowlands left few stelae from this Postclassic Period. Surviving inscriptions tend to be on stone lintels and wall panels. They do not portray great kings and tell their life histories. Instead, they use few pictures and celebrate fire rites and the dedication of buildings. It seems there was not any dynasty to celebrate.

These inscriptions refer to shared rule by a council of up to four people.

The writing in the four surviving Maya codices mainly concerns priestly rituals and tables for calculating astronomical events. Writing on carved bones and jade and on the pots and other ceramic goods left with deceased royals and nobles in their graves mostly gives the name and titles of the deceased and sometimes also contains dedications to the gods. Some also name the artist who drew them.

Below: Maya stonecut glyphs from stele M at Copán. It honours the city's 15th king, Smoke Shell, who completed Copán's Hieroglyphic Stairway. The stair has 2,500 glyphs listing the kings of the ruling dynasty.

FRAGMENTS OF HISTORY

The Spanish missionaries who arrived in Maya lands after the conquest of Tenochtitlán were responsible for burning many of the locals' bark-paper books or codices. One of the most enthusiastic of these was Bishop Diego de Landa, author of *Report of Things in Yucatán*, who wrote, 'These people used certain letters with which they wrote in their books about ancient subjects … We found many books written with these letters and since they held nothing that was not falsehood and the work of the evil one, we burned them all'.

THE CODICES

As far as we know, only four Maya codices survived the attentions of the monks. Three of these codices are now known after the names of the European cities in which they are kept – the Dresden, Madrid and Paris Codices – while the fourth, the *Grolier Codex*, is in North America. They contain many images of Maya deities, as well as information used by priests for divining the future, timing sacred rituals and monitoring the movements of Venus and the eclipses of the sun and moon.

THE POPOL VUH

Other surviving accounts of Maya history and mythology were written down after the Conquest. The *Popol Vuh* ('Book of Advice') was a sacred text of the Quiché, a group of southern Maya inhabiting highland Guatemala. It survived for posterity through a combination of Quiché determination and good fortune. The original book, in Maya hieroglyphs, was secretly translated into the Roman alphabet by members of the Quiché nobility in the mid-1500s. This was part of an attempt to preserve the book at a time when the Spaniards, who had conquered the region in 1523–24, were seeking to exterminate native culture. The manuscript was not found until later in the century, by which time some members of the Catholic Church had begun to see some merit in recording and preserving accounts of ancient Mesoamerican culture and history and so allowed it to be preserved. This version was discovered in 1703 by Francisco Ximenez, a Franciscan friar who could read Quiché and who was therefore able to translate the text into Spanish.

Left: This funerary urn was used by the Quiché, southern Guatemalan Maya, whose holy book, the Popol Vuh, *contains a detailed account of the creation of the world.*

Above: An unknown 4th-century Maya ruler adorns a jade belt pendant found in the Petén region.

NATIVE HISTORIES

Two other native histories survive. The first, *The Annals of the Cakchiquels*, contains entries up to 1604 and describes the history of the Cakchiquels, neighbours of the Quiché, from mythical beginnings onwards. Like the *Popol Vuh*, it was first transcribed into the Roman alphabet in the 1500s. The second, *The Books of Chilam Balam*, contains a mixture

Right: Spanish conquistadors prepare to land in Mexico in 1519. The invaders' unfortunate belief that the local books and religious rites were wicked led to a terrible cultural loss.

of prophecy and history-myth of the Maya of Yucatán. These accounts were kept from the early 16th century onwards, but were rewritten, with additions, until the 19th century. They take their name from a Maya seer who is said to have predicted the coming of 'bearded men of the east' who would bring violence and force the Maya to speak another language. Both these sources give eyewitness accounts of the Spanish conquest and the many changes that followed it.

Below: Information concerning Maya cosmology and details of the gods associated with the four principal directions are to be found in the Madrid Codex.

INDEX

PICTURE ACKNOWLEDGEMENTS

The Art Archive: 73bl, /Bodleian Library, Oxford: 71b, 105b, /Dagli Orti: 14t, 20b, 28t, 44t, 53l, 55b, 56t, 57b, 62, 71t, 72b, 73t, 75t, 78, 79t, 80b, 84b, 85b, 88l and r, 89b, 90l, 94l, 95b, 101b, 105t, 110b, 120r, 121l, 122b, 129t, 131t, 137b, 138t, 139b, /Eileen Tweedy: 49b, /Mireille Vautier: 63b, 69b, 77t, 80t, 106–7, 125t. **The Bridgeman Art Library**: 29t, 55t, 69t, 76t, 96l, 97, 99t, 104l, 119t, /Archives Charmet: 58b, /Giraudon: 27t, 116r, /Index: 94tr, /Lauros/Giraudon: 92, /IanMursell/Mexicolore: 24t, /Banco Mexicano de Imagenes/INAH: 74, 99r, /The Stapleton Collection: 93t and b. **Corbis**: 108l, /Archivo Iconografico, S.A.: 96r, 114–5, /Anna Clopet: 83t, /Randy Faris: 41t, /Arvind Garg: 35b, /Kimbell Art Museum: 91b, /Danny Lehman: 58t, /Charles and Josette Lenars: 22t and b, 68t, /Macduff Everton: 95t, Gianni Dagli Orti: 11l, 16t, 23l and r, 42t, 43b, 54b, 75b, 84t, 85t, 102r, 103tr and b, Enzo & Paolo Ragazzini: 34b, /Nick Wheeler: 76b. **Werner Forman**: 52b, 63t, 100tr, 112t, 118b, /David Bernstein, New York: 52t, 101t, /Biblioteca Nacional, Madrid: 27t, /Biblioteca Universitaria, Bologna: 61, 70b, 108t, 113t /British Museum, London: 28b, 48, 56b, 60b, /Dallas Museum of Art: 64l, 100b, /Field Museum of

Natural History, Chicago: 70m, /Liverpool Museum, Liverpool: 49t, /Edward H. Merrin Gallery, New York: 90r, /Museo de America, Madrid: 117t, /Museum of the Americas, New York: 125b, /Museum of Fine Arts, Dallas: 98l, /Museum für Völkerkunde, Basle: 24b, 53r, 122t, /Museum für Völkerkunde, Berlin: 57t, 59tr, 116l, /Museum für Völkerkunde, Vienna: 25t, /National Museum of Anthropology, Mexico: 68b, 77b, 81b, 83b, 109tl and r, 123t, /Pigorini Museum of Prehistory and Ethnography, Rome: 27b, 54t, 72r, /Portland Art Museum, Oregon: 104t, /private collection: 20t, /private collection, London: 34t, /private collection, Mexico City: 89t, /private collection, New York: 81r, 90l, 118t, 120l, 124r, /Smithsonian Institution, Washington: 110t, /Dr Kurt Stavanenhagen Collection, Mexico City: 45b. **N.J. Saunders**: 10tr, 18t, 25b, 30–1, 35t, 36b. **South American Pictures**: /Robert Francis: 10tl, 16br, 21b, 32t, 36t, 39t, 44b, 45t, /Tony Morrison: 11tr, 12–3, 14l, 15b, 19t and b, 29b, 32bl, 37l, 40t, 41b, 46–7, 60t, 66–7, 86–7, 98r, 111t, 122r, /Chris Sharp: 11bl, 15t, 16bl, 18b, 21t, 37r, 38l and r, 39b, 40b, 42b, 59tl, 64r, 65t and b, 79b, 82l and r, 102l, 23b, /Rebecca Whitfield: 32br.